Praise for *The Pi

"If you're interested in the relationship between artistic creativity and psychic health (and who isn't?), this is a book you will come back to many times. Margret Elson has a deep understanding of these connections, and she explores them in compassionate and engaging prose. Why do so many creative people have periods of unproductivity? What can a wise and caring therapist do to help them? This is a book as engaging as it is original, as original as it is profound."

— **Robin Lakoff**, PhD, professor of linguistics emerita, UC Berkeley; author of *Language and Woman's Place*, *Talking Power*, and *Context Counts*

"Margret Elson is a master musician, performer and teacher. In her previous book Passionate Practice: The Musician's Guide to Learning, Memorizing and Performing *— a book that has received much attention and acclaim — she has written cogently about attaining optimum performance for musicians. But she is also a trained psychotherapist. Reading this book, we gain an understanding of how teaching is therapeutic. Elson gives us a wonderful, heartwarming and eminently readable account of her own experiences in this special arena."*

— **Paul Sheftel**, pianist, teacher, former faculty member at the Juilliard School, and piano editor for Carl Fischer

"Elson integrates bodywork, psychodynamic, gestalt and Jungian techniques in her unique approach to self-discovery at the keyboard and in life. As a psychologist who loves piano, I would put Elson's book at the top of my reading list for graduate students studying the subtleties and complexities of psychotherapy

— **Nadine M. Payn**, PhD, former psychology talk-radio host, KGO Radio, San Francisco

"This book is a celebration of the harmony between the mental and physical aspects of the person. Elson, a musician and a teacher of musicians, recognizes that mental and physical states should be integrated into a single music-creating being. She writes: 'The body is a brain that moves.' This book includes three extended clinical examples of putting these ideas into practice. I found these examples illuminating and provocative."

— **Dr. Sandra Bemesderfer**, psychologist and psychoanalyst

The Piano and the Couch

MUSIC AND PSYCHE

MARGRET ELSON

Janowski-Tell Publishers
Oakland, California

Published by

Janowski-Tell Publishers

Oakland, California

ISBN: 978-0-9991174-1-5 (hardcover)

ISBN: 978-0-9991174-0-8 (softcover)

Cover and interior design: Vicky Vaughn Shea, Ponderosa Pine Design

Publishing strategist: Holly Brady, HollyBrady.com

Author photo: Rod Searcey, RodSearcey.com

Other books by this author:

Passionate Practice: The Musician's Guide to Learning, Memorizing and Performing

Address permission requests to:

info@PianoAndCouch.com

For information on purchasing multiple copies of this book at reduced prices, please inquire at info@PianoAndCouch.com

This book is dedicated to the students and clients who have given me the opportunity to sit with them and listen to their music, listen to their stories. In the process, they have taught me much about myself.

CONTENTS

SECTION IV: Terms & Exercises

A Few Words about Dialogue and Quotes

Throughout the book there is extensive use of dialogue between myself and clients. Dialogues and quotes are taken from actual conversations, which I usually recorded immediately after or, in rare instances, during sessions. Quotes from other people and tapes are taken verbatim from their material.

Though the case narratives are naturally abridged, I have felt it necessary to present them somewhat fully, given the intensity and richness of the material as well as the fact that our work progressed along parallel paths of music and psychology, reflecting the unusual nature of the work.

TEACH ME SO I CAN STUDY WITH SOMEONE ELSE

When I was in my early thirties and had been teaching piano for four years—and therefore considered myself an expert!—I received a call from a student that subsequently changed my life.

Twenty-one-year-old David S. was an engineering student at the university and wanted to change his major to music. His musical experience included singing in choirs and reading the treble clef on the piano. But two years of engineering studies had brought a change of heart, and, after much self-questioning, David decided that music was his calling. The first step toward that goal was passing qualifying exams in performing at the university so that he could study piano as a music major. He had six months in which to prepare. He obtained my name from the music department's list of teachers outside the university. When he called me he announced that, once accepted into the department, he would change teachers to study with one at the university. And starting with that call I was, albeit unconsciously, on the defensive.

David came for his first lesson: tall, dark-complexioned, a brooding personality; large, beautiful piano hands; a love of music; a yearning to play the piano; and one thing more—a surly manner. Despite thinking I knew everything about teaching, our lessons became increasingly difficult for me, and it became clear that I wasn't helping David.

In addition to teaching him the art of playing the piano, I wanted David to benefit from the full panoply of my musical knowledge: theory, sight-reading, and comparisons of different interpretations. He countered me on every front.

"That's not what I want," he would say. "I just want to learn to play the pieces." The more he challenged me, the more entrenched I became in identifying myself in the role of teacher, the authority. I simply wasn't getting it.

In desperation I consulted Susan, a music therapist, on how to break through to my student. She suggested that she and I role-play. When I took on the role of David, I readily balked when Susan, role-playing me, steered me to look at the piece from a structural point of view.

"I don't want to do that. I only want to learn to play the piece," I said petulantly, overplaying my role. When she attended to teaching me the piece at hand, I settled down and listened.

As my frustrated teacher-self, I tried cajoling Susan, now role-playing David, into looking at the phrasing structure.

"That will help in understanding the piece and learning it better," I asserted.

When we finished role-playing, Susan spoke candidly. "He told you from the beginning what he wants: He wants you to help him learn some pieces for the performing exam. Nothing more. What are you trying to accomplish?"

I got it. I was in a power play. It was fueled by David's initial declaration that he was going to use me, then dump me for an in-house teacher—that's how it felt. It was reinforced by the fact that he was the essence of the brooding-artist type I had always found attractive, and by my embarrassment at *feeling* dumpy at a fat eight months into my pregnancy. I was fighting him to salvage my own self-worth and dignity. Miraculous though it may seem, the instant Susan pulled the blinders from my eyes I was able to let go of the need to control him and took control of myself instead. I finally became the piano teacher I had contracted to become when I accepted David as a student, giving him my best to achieve *his* goal.

David passed his piano performance exam, playing a Brahms intermezzo and a Chopin etude. It was quite an accomplishment for us both, considering that he had come to me a mere six months earlier with rudimentary piano skills. As promised (or threatened, as I had felt), he switched to a teacher at the university, thanking me for our work together.

It was I, however, who was indebted to him. David had made me aware that music lessons are about more than learning music. They involve a complicated relationship between the participating parties. We had skirted disaster: Had I not been motivated to seek help, he would have experienced, at the very least, one miserable relationship with one obstinate and clueless piano teacher. Who knows how that might have colored his continuing music education? I wondered: What do other students and teachers experience, without awareness, in this intense relationship?

Such questions provided the fertile soil for what was to become my new profession. I was going to become a . . . ? I didn't know a term for it. Someone who, when presented with a problem by a musician, could dissect it as either a musical or a nonmusical issue, or perhaps both, and could then provide appropriate guidance. Not exactly a therapist, not exactly a teacher, and not a music therapist. I created the term Artistic Counselor, and that's what I became. I had a second career in addition to teaching piano, and I had David to thank for it.

Several years later David called.

"Hi. This is David S. . . . Do you remember me?" Indeed I did.

"I just wanted to let you know what's been happening." It was a much softer, mature voice at the other end. "After graduation I went back home to the Midwest, where I now have a large music studio. I'm teaching mostly young children and some adults." There was a moment's pause.

"I also just want you to know I've come to appreciate how much I learned from you and in such a short period of time. I haven't learned that much from any teacher since. I was always sorry I didn't stay. . . . And how are *you?*"

Wiser, much wiser, I thought, smiling to myself.

When I look back on that experience more than forty years ago, I view that initial failure as a gift that kick-started my own search for wholeness. It forced me to confront my personal demons, and to find meaning in individual steps of the trajectory of my life. It forced me to question myself as well as my assumptions, and to recognize that when we work on music we are working on ourselves.

David's appearance played out a classical literary narrative, in which a stranger appears briefly in someone's life, then disappears, leaving that life vastly changed. His appearance was the catalyst for my forging an alliance between my professional calling as a musician and my instinctual need for psychological probing and understanding. It led me to return to school to get a master's degree in clinical psychology and become a licensed psychotherapist. It resulted in my having dual careers as pianist and psychotherapist, and being able to create a unique space between the piano and the couch to access the ineffable yearning of the soul.

The search for wholeness is ongoing. Demons of self-doubt and harsh judgment may never go away completely. But moments of redemption appear, as well. Together, demons and redemption provide the meaning that allows us to continue seeking. This book gives a glimpse into the ideas and stories that evolved from working with clients and students at couch and piano, and shows how the search for wholeness brings its own surprises.

THE SEARCH FOR WHOLENESS AT PIANO AND COUCH

[ONE]

MUSIC AND PSYCHE - SOULMATES

The individual life is made significant by the struggle.

— Eugene O'Neill

Celeste pivoted on the piano bench as her lesson ended and faced me sitting in my chair next to her.

"Before I fully awoke this morning I had a dream about coming here. There was a couch next to the piano, but you were sitting in your teacher's chair and I was sitting here at the piano just having a piano lesson."

"What a graphic depiction of the title I'm thinking of giving the book I'm writing! We talked about it last week."

"Yes, I remember you mentioned writing, but you never mentioned a title."

But, of course, I hadn't needed to. The couch Celeste had dreamed about was symbolic of the emotional work that had taken place in conjunction with her lessons over the past five years, all of it part of the search for her musical being. The emotional (couch) work had often overshadowed the musical (piano) work, for it had become clear soon after we started working together that her inability to progress at the piano was emblematic of the deep despair embedded in her psyche. Musical instruction could not nourish her musical growth while energy was being siphoned off by festering emotional issues.

As a piano teacher as well as a psychotherapist, I well know the distinctions between teaching and therapy. Yet there are striking similarities between them.

Both endeavors are challenging and demand time and patience, as well as *practice, practice, practice.* Each is a quest for mastery, over oneself or over an instrument. In my studio, it is in the sacred space between couch and piano where that mastery is often achieved.

In that space, Celeste and I traversed her world of anguish, abandonment and abuse, all in the pursuit of playing piano. It was there she turned to making music unaccompanied by punitive parents, putative heart attacks, narcissistic teachers, and dragons. Neither of us could have foreseen what would unfold when she originally called, saying: "I'm not sure what to do about my music. Maybe we could talk."

We talked, and we did much more. Celeste's search for her musician-self (see chapter 3, "Celeste – The Dragon and Debussy") was irrevocably intertwined with her search for her whole self. It was imperative to engage in reparative work that moved between musical and nonmusical arenas, and between verbal and nonverbal approaches in order to heal the underlying psychic wounds that erupted at the piano. As a symbol of those wounds for Celeste, the presence of the piano served as a potent catalyst for the work; even when it stood idle, it could not be ignored.

Music, Daniel Barenboim writes, "teaches us, in short, that everything is connected."[1] The quest for wholeness is not only about connecting to our truest self, and to the integrity experienced when we act in concert with that self. It is also about the integrity of our connections to others, to the stuff of our lives—our daily activities, our work, our art—as well as to the cosmic forces outside ourselves, however such forces are personally perceived.

This quest for wholeness and connection is universal, and many are the pathways one can traverse toward their attainment. The paths with which I am most familiar personally and professionally are the worlds of music and psychology. In this book you will read case studies detailing journeys on those paths and get a glimpse of how closely the process of discovery at couch and piano resemble one another.

Music and psyche are soulmates, siblings sharing vital compartments in our being. The writer George Eliot called the ear—the organ through which music is transmitted—"that delicate messenger to the inmost sanctuary of the soul."[2] The power of music derives from its direct impact on our nerves, needing no further cognitive interpretation. It can be compared to the direct and unmediated impact of preverbal, preconscious experience on the body. Music has the same emotional impact on the same private domain within our psyche that houses our deepest human emotions: joy, sorrow, fear, hope, disappointment. Author Diane Ackerman posits that human beings, from the beginning of history, "required music to add meaning to their lives."[3]

"Tears open gates, but music breaks down walls" is an old Hassidic saying.[4] And you will read how potent is the image of walls in several of the case studies in this book. Music is a powerful tool both in calming the spirit and in awakening it. In my studio I have witnessed agitated clients calm themselves by listening to a favorite piece of music, or sing to themselves to quiet disturbing inner voices. The piano virtuoso Glenn Gould reportedly hummed to himself instead of crying when he fell down.[5]

Music though has power not only to calm, but to disturb as well. When my father died, I found myself unable to listen to music. We had been very close, and it was from him that I received my talent and love for music. Listening to music after he died overwhelmed me emotionally. Its lack in my life was less painful than the pain it elicited. When my mother died, however, music helped me realize the full extent of my grief, bridging the emotional gap I had experienced with her in life, and reminding me of the constancy of her love. Her death brought us closer at the same time it brought me sorrow, and a longing to make amends.

Our deepest sense of ourselves, of our loved ones, of our place in the world and of our spiritual yearnings—these most primordial attributes of being human—are lodged in our psyche and expressed in music. "The power of music lies in its ability to speak to all aspects of the human being—the animal, the emotional, the intellectual and the spiritual," to quote Barenboim again.[6] Psychology, too, deals with the whole human being: mind, spirit and body. It therefore feels natural and organic to me that I practice both careers of musician and therapist, borrowing from one to enhance the other, and applying the metaphors that link music and psyche.

Many people intuitively grasp the natural link between music and psyche. When Eduardo, a violinist, called asking for therapy, he said simply: "I heard you play Chopin at your recital last week. I knew right away you would be the right therapist."

But Raymond, a pianist feeling emotionally unable to access his passion for music, viewed the teacher/therapist combination with ambiguity. As he entered my studio for the first time, he declared: "I'm not sure what I'm doing here. You're also a therapist, aren't you? I don't believe in therapy. It doesn't work. I just want to work on the music." Without replying, I followed him as he walked over to the piano and sat down.

For the next four months, he came in and strode directly to the piano, then sat there without playing a note. But he talked: about his childhood, about its punitive environment, about getting locked in closets, being hit for speaking out and shamed for wanting to play the piano. Sitting safely next to his instrument allowed Raymond to revisit old wounds, which he seemed compelled to do before he could unlock his music. As I listened closely, I didn't mention that the work he was engaging in while sitting at the piano was therapy.

Though the conscious motivation for studying music differs from that of seeking therapy, the quest for wholeness underpins both endeavors. In that quest, similar themes emerge, among which are the search both for a meaningful life and for emotional and spiritual nourishment. Listen to the following voices of piano students and therapy clients:

I long to recover my spirituality as a musician. I once had it but no more. Music is my salvation, but at the same time I've become disconnected from it and its power to heal.

— Piano student

I feel empty inside, disconnected from my soul, the part that makes me who I am. I seem to be filled with everyone but myself.

— Therapy client

I dreamed I was in front of the big glass windows of a restaurant looking in. I saw everyone eating at these elegant tables, linen tablecloths and silver and crystal. Feeling I couldn't enter such a restaurant I went around the back instead, where the kitchen was, looking for a place to eat. From there I saw into the main dining room and realized it was really your studio. I

was upset that I still couldn't allow myself the privilege of coming in the
front door to be where I wanted to be. At the piano. Just being me.

— Piano student

I dreamed I was in a restaurant and the waiter brought my meal, but when
I tasted it, it wasn't quite right. I didn't say anything. But then my husband
took a bite from my plate. He immediately called the waiter over and in a
calm voice said to take it back. Once again I realized that I hadn't followed
my instincts and had let someone else take care of me. When will I learn to
use my own voice?

— Therapy client

The longing for wholeness manifested at couch or piano—through dreams of nourishment, through yearning for spirituality—is a basic human striving, one as old as the human race itself.

"In all life there is longing. Creation itself is a longing," intoned a rabbi at the Jewish New Year service of Rosh Hashanah. The creation story speaks of man's separation from unity with the Biblical god and paradise. Down on earth that story is mirrored in the baby's separation from the original mother–child uterine paradise. From the very moment we are born, we become seekers, longing for that original connection. As we mature, we continue seeking: by expanding our knowledge of ourselves and of the world, and through our relationships with others, our work and our art. "Music evokes an existence beyond this one, toward which the soul inexpressibly yearns."[7] And in the process of yearning, we continually confront ourselves.

Yearning for connection to something larger than ourselves, like music or spirituality, is a complex phenomenon, often defying description. The longed-for state has been compared to that of womblike subliminal, and effortless well-being. When yearning achieves such an organic connection, it might be called ecstasy, even orgasmic, being *in the zone*. Chamber music played as if by one performer. Oarsmen in "swing" when everyone in the boat rows effortlessly in sync.[8] But underneath the yearning might lurk the fear—one that the creative artist in any field instinctively understands—of an unconscious pull toward an undifferentiated, oceanic state in which our separate individuality is subsumed into boundless

23

infinity. A felt danger of disappearing into the void. That was the fear, I believe, that stopped me from listening to music after my father died: the fear of disappearing into the vortex of grief and being unable to return.

Disappearing may seem too strong a word. But working at couch or piano involves working with strong emotions. I often hear how the anxiety of disappearing prevents this student or that client from fully engaging with strong emotions lest they be swallowed up by them. This trepidation also stymies their effort at finding their own voice by putting a brake on the process. It is a complicated and delicate issue, like human endeavors often are.

The challenge most fraught in the search for meaning and wholeness is that of confronting ourselves and our personal demons—those parts of ourselves that are entrenched in preventing us from moving forward. They may include even those positive traits we prefer to overlook because of early contamination—for example, being told that smart girls are unattractive. We worry constantly about being exposed as *less than*, unworthy, a fraud, vain or self-important.

"And the painfulness of rejection never grows less. In our hearts, we are all six years old," declared Brendan Gill of *The New Yorker* fame.[9] Fear of exposing our most intimate self can be tantamount to despair for those whose personal identity and self-worth are identified with product or performance.

Author David Benioff underscores this point dramatically in his novel about Saint Petersburg under siege during World War II. Kolya, a young soldier in the novel, secretly yearns to write, but "the fear of fully disclosing himself is more daunting than war. Cannibals and Nazis didn't make Kolya nervous, but the threat of embarrassment did—the possibility that a stranger might laugh at the lines he'd written."[10]

The Demagogue Within

My own demon surfaced when, after years of talk therapy, I began a body-oriented therapy. Talking had brought many positive changes in my life, but I had hit a wall in dislodging firmly entrenched beliefs that held me back, and my gracious, wise therapist suggested a change.

As I spoke with my new body-oriented therapist about my upbringing, I mentioned how difficult it had been for my father, who had lost his family in the

Holocaust, and with whom I was so close, to tolerate a difference of opinion with me, actually calling me a "demagogue" when I disagreed with him. Later I would realize how frightening it must have been for my father when I disagreed with him: by separating myself from him, if only in opinion, I may have unconsciously activated his fear of losing me, as he had his family in Europe. But as an adolescent I experienced his behavior as encroaching on my right to self-expression. In time, I grew increasingly reticent to express myself, for unconsciously my own self-assertion became intertwined with the fear of demolishing my father.

My new therapist asked me to lie on my back on the floor and, arms by my sides, pound my fists while exclaiming, "I am *not* a demagogue, I am *not* a demagogue." I followed his instructions with as much conviction as I could muster, trying to negate my father's statement, but it felt forced and ineffectual.

That segued into declaring the following: "I *am* a demagogue, I *am* a demagogue." That registered! On making this positive assertion, and ironically agreeing with my father, energy burst forth in my body. As energy flowed through newfound internal tributaries, it was exhilarating to discover a newfound attribute to my personality: the ability to be self-assertive, and the realization that simply possessing that attribute did not make me like Hitler, the idea of whom was undoubtedly lodged in my father's unconscious. It took time to fully understand and incorporate this event into the fabric of my being, but this exercise taught me important lessons that eventually informed not only my self-image but my professional work as well.

At a visceral level, I "got" the import of accepting what Carl Jung called our shadow side, the part of ourselves that is undeveloped or unwelcome, that is in some way regarded as inappropriate or unattractive. For me, the "demagogue" was the part of me with separate opinions from my father. It was the physical—rather than intellectual—assertion that I *was* that forbidden aspect that helped me reclaim an essential piece of my wholeness and in the process release energy. As sociologist Susan Phillips states in her book *Candlelight*: "The antithesis of fear is not certainty, but . . . vitality."[11]

The shadow side contains huge resources of energy. If denied or unrecognized, we risk dangerous acting-out against others, as evidenced daily in accounts of rampant rage by ordinary people. Unrecognized, the shadow's power can poison our inner world.

Clients and students have their own idiosyncratic names for the demon, like my demagogue, who prohibits their freedom of expression. One woman called hers "Darth Vader," another "The Dragon." One actor called his "Brando," another "Selfish One." Alexander called his, the "Plague" (see chapter 4, "Alexander – A Trinity of Selves"). A gay client's demon was the refrain of a childhood taunt: "Faggy." Other shadow names I've heard include Arrogant, Unladylike, Haughty, Show-Off, Diva and Warrior. Such were the descriptions given to their personal demons by people taught to suppress behavior that might be viewed askance. Such demonized attributes siphon off energy from the life-giving force that results when we are connected to all parts of ourselves. The goal, therefore, whether at couch or at piano, is to find the most natural way to uncover and reconnect with this vitality.

Like many people seeking connection through music or therapy, the people in this book found it necessary to confront their early experiences. When such confrontations are powerful, and especially if they are traumatic, they may precipitate regression to a client's earlier age. In safe, supportive surroundings, these are necessary reversions. It often happens that those earlier selves experienced some form of abuse. It needs to be said that abuse is subjectively experienced, and, as you will read, levels of abuse may be mild to severe. A person's subjective experience, along with his or her basic character, contributes to how that individual responds. As there is considerable literature about abuse, I shall not write extensively about it here. There are, however, characteristics that appear in the narratives in this book that need addressing.

Despite the lack of culpability on the part of an abused child, that child will invariably feel guilty. When parents have inflicted abuse, the child often needs the ironically comforting fantasy that he was responsible for and deserving of it. Then the child can hold onto the unrealistic expectation that he has some control in the process, that if only the right way to behave could be found things would improve: *If I were good, my mother (father) would like me better; if I didn't ask for a new toy, I wouldn't get punished.*

Unfortunately, there is seldom certainty about what constitutes good behavior. Abusive parents exist in their own world of deprivation and denial, and respond irrationally. Not knowing what behavior will elicit retribution, the fear of punishment permeates the child's existence. Such fear is panic-driven and generalized.

Not being able to distinguish between degrees of transgression, any stepping out of line—like not understanding what the parent (later, the piano teacher) says or wants, or making a mistake at the table (or at the music lesson)—is experienced as possible cause for punishment. Long after those responsible for abusive behavior are gone, their primitive powers persist and other people continue to be viewed in the grown child's mind as potential agents of abuse. Thus, the fear of its recurrence remains present.

Conversely, the abused person may unconsciously pull for its recurrence in the classic repetition compulsion to which we are all subject. It is a most human endeavor, to satisfy our physical and psychic need for the familiar by repeating old patterns. Thus, you will witness how Celeste (see chapter 3, "Celeste – The Dragon and Debussy") both fears punishment from me—for not performing as a good piano student—yet appears to pull for a punishing response—by not performing as a good student. Shame is constant in the life of an abused person: shame about what happened in the past, shame for not knowing or achieving something in the present, whether or not it is a realistic expectation. "I should just know," they tell themselves.

When someone lives through an unendurable experience, the dissociation—that is, the splitting of his personality into component parts—serves as a protective mechanism. When normal regulatory mechanisms used for coping are overwhelmed, emotional segments may get fragmented, split into separate selves or identities called "alters." Alters often represent aspects of a person's personality or emotions like anger, neediness or self-expression that were unheeded or forbidden expression.

In dissociated minds, mental barriers can arise between the experience of each compartmentalized alter, inhibiting them from developing ways of reasonably dealing with their emotions. An alter stuck in rage, for example, will not be able to learn how to modify behavior from the rational part; the needy alter will not learn how to fulfill its needs. These selves remain developmentally static, always angry, always needy.

The above traits are not peculiar to victims of abuse. We all need to be cared for as children, want to be loved throughout our lives, and sometimes feel shame, guilt, fear. To some degree, we compartmentalize our attention when we daydream, perform repetitive tasks or watch television. What distinguishes normal from problematic compartmentalizing is the degree of separation from cognition, and the level of despair that ensues when emotional segmentation prevents someone from moving forward in his life.

The Body Is a Brain

We are in the midst of a revolution in recognizing that mind, body and emotions are more elegantly intertwined than traditionally regarded in Western thought. Increasingly, attention is being paid by neurologists, psychologists and musicians, among others, to the importance of the body in learning, holding memories and making music. Science continually unveils the "mysteries" of music-making, showing how it affects and activates every emotional system of the brain and how deeply physical music-making actually is.

> *Virtually every culture and civilization considers movement to be an integral part of music making and listening. . . . Making music requires that energy be transmitted from body movements to a musical instrument in a coordinated, rhythmic use of our bodies. At a neural level, playing an instrument requires the orchestration of regions in our primitive, reptilian brain—the cerebellum and the brain stem—as well as higher cognitive systems such as the motor cortex (in the parietal lobe) and the planning regions of our frontal lobes, the most advanced region of the brain.[12]*

That is to say, music originates in movement, and making music results from coordinating regions of the brain responsible for movement with those regions responsible for thinking and planning. To make music, then, we must honor nature's design of music-making as an integrated brain/body activity. Increasing recognition is being given to this idea, and movement is increasingly being incorporated in musical education.

Richard Leppert, a philosopher of music and society, writes eloquently about the relation of music to the body: "Whatever else music is 'about,' it is *inevitably* about the body; music's aural and visual presence constitutes both a relation to and a representation of the body."[13] Also: "Music's pleasure is the temporary 'realignment' of body with mind. . . ."[14] However, Leppert illustrates how the legacy bequeathed us by Western tradition—from early Greek thought through the Enlightenment—which elevates mind over embodied experience, militates against his thesis. And until recently, our legacy has precluded incorporating the fullness of body experience into the discovery processes at work in psychology and music.

The practice of psychotherapy of necessity acknowledges the ability of the body to communicate. Therapists readily read clients' body language and facial expressions as clues to their state of mind. I have found, in addition, that more-active movements, such as walking, dancing and assuming body postures, can be profoundly informative in unleashing meaning and emotion both at couch and in music-making. Even bullfighting teaches this lesson: "Dance with the bull," a three-time world champion bullfighter declares, adding: "Never try to fight; if you fight, you always lose."[15] Movement, yes; fighting, no.

[TWO]

HOW PIANO AND COUCH
INFORM EACH OTHER

A dynamic and graphic introduction to how piano and couch inform each other comes from Sydney, a student of mine in his forties, an accomplished musician and a therapist with a traditional practice.

At a piano lesson one day, Sydney related an upsetting interchange with his closest friend, also a pianist. Feeling—perhaps wrongly, he admitted—that his friend had denigrated his musicality, Sydney was so deflated that he could not practice that week. Almost in tears, he berated himself for being reduced to feeling like a youngster. "Imagine! At my age, a few off-hand comments and I forget I have talent. . . . I couldn't even practice; my passion just disappeared."

Unsure how a traditional therapist would receive a nontraditional suggestion, I nevertheless asked if he was willing to do an exercise, and he agreed. I led him through the breathing exercise I call the Automatic Relax Response. (See Section IV, Terms & Exercises for more information on the exercises discussed throughout this book.) For several minutes, he focused attention on breathing to his abdomen. His body automatically released energy held by the upper body. When Sydney appeared calmer, I suggested that he allow a picture to appear at the spot to which he was breathing. Without hesitating, Sydney closed his eyes and in a few moments said he saw a picture of himself as a little boy looking forlorn, just as he remembered feeling at that age. I suggested that he envision taking the little boy's hand and reassuring the child that he would not leave him. "You understand how he feels," I said, "and he needs your strength and guidance. You need each other now."

31

Sydney was quiet and, opening his eyes, silently wiped away the tears. Slowly, he turned back to the piano and asked if we could play four-hands together.

The following week, Sydney sat down, his eyes twinkling. "When I left here last week, I went right to my office, still sensing my little boy. The first client I saw is extremely depressed, and as she lay on the couch she talked about how empty she feels, how meaningless her life is. I flashed on my telling you about how my own passion was failing me, and asked about *her* passion, a question I'd never asked before. She said she had none. Then, I did something else I never do—I asked her to close her eyes while lying on the couch. When she did I repeated the question, and right away she listed things she loved—painting, writing, gardening . . . she'd never discussed those before. It was new for both of us, and it came directly out of opening up to myself here at the piano."

I thought of the beauty in the circle being inscribed: couch work that had occurred at the piano in my studio brought back by Sydney to couch work in *his* office. There, he allowed the discovery of *his* passion to pave the way for his client to explore her own.

Breathing and Movement

The immediate impetus for Sydney's breakthrough was the breathing exercise and envisioning an internal image, an image that becomes a cue to relax. It is all about movement, in this case the internal movement of breathing, the release of energy and the conscious shifting of focus. Movement means continuity. Music is the movement of continual vibrations, carrying us forward through sound and silence, and activating interior kinesthetic vibrations of emotion. At the couch of self-discovery, finding oneself fully alive entails an alert body and mind. It implies that energy flows not only between body and mind, but equally importantly between past and present, the present moment being the confluence of all antecedent moments. The free flow of energy is dammed when part of one's past is denied or repressed. Life has no fluidity when trauma, for example, interferes with natural development. However, physical movement can access that energy, as occurred when I pounded my fists on the floor. Energy, once freed, can manifest in remarkable shapes, as the following story shows.

I was giving a workshop in London called "Overcoming Creative Blocks."

While I worked with Ron on his fear of auditioning for a singing role, I noticed Dory sitting on the sidelines softly crying. I asked her to join the group.

"I don't have anything to work on," she sighed, then paused, seemingly searching for something appropriate to discuss. "I took music lessons as a youngster but they were horrible so I don't play anymore." Since she mentioned music I pursued her thought, hoping to find an entrée for her into the group.

"Lessons were all so rigid," she replied. "'Learn this piece. Now learn this one. Don't make mistakes. Don't look at your hands.' Nothing else. I was little; I was always afraid. I think I was crying just now because Ron suddenly came alive and belted out that song. I'd never be that free."

But she was willing to try my suggestions. Describing her experience in an article for a British psychotherapy journal a year later, she wrote:

> *The exercise Margret devised for me was a pretend performance, crashing about the keyboard at will, with no regard for the actual notes being played. This I did with due ceremony. The lack of prohibition struck a deep chord in me, tears flowed, the audience applauded and my performance ended. I never bothered much about the piano afterwards, but nine months later my daughter was born.*

The remarkable part was that she and her partner had been trying to have a child for seven years without success. The uninhibited movement she had experienced in the workshop clearly released energy, which then found its own appropriate channel of creativity.

Holding the view that the mind and body belong together, and that they should both participate in becoming an integrated whole at the couch or piano, entails having a broad outlook and range of approaches. The means used to pursue such a task need to be commensurate with the task itself: rich, varied and multilayered, for such is the holistic view of each individual. The mind-set of the guide needs to be fluid, not rigid like a demagogue's!

The poet Mallarmé wrote in 1867:

> *I think the healthy thing for man—for reflective nature—is to think with his whole body; then you get a full harmonious thought, like the violin strings*

vibrating in union. . . . When thoughts come from the brain alone . . . they are like tunes played on the squeaky part of the first string. . . . They come and go . . . without leaving any trace.[16]

Musicians know that music-making is the accretion of numberless hours of practice. Teachers may not always address the fullness of the body in their attention to the technical demands of playing—this, despite exhortations of master teachers, such as the following:

Musicality is a physical expression.

— Pablo Casals, in a recorded interview

If you keep your body relaxed, the body is in contact with the depths of your soul.

— Claudio Arrau[17]

Play from the inside out.

— Margaret Rowell, famed cello teacher

Play fully; let the music rise from your feet through your torso.

— Phyllis Lehrer, internationally recognized pianist and professor of piano studies, Westminster Choir College[18]

In producing good sound, the lower body, the legs and abdomen are essential.

— Sviatoslav Richter[19]

The body imitates music . . . and . . . the music that one produces will inevitably imitate the bodily state.

— Charles Rosen, pianist and music critic[20]

Cellists and other instrumentalists hold their instrument, and thus understand the connection between themselves and their instrument by virtue of its contiguity to their body. Their instruments become extensions of their bodies, breathing and moving in tandem. In contrast, pianists facing their huge instrument often consider their relationship as adversarial: conquer or be conquered. Creating a natural connection between pianist and piano entails harnessing breathing, the senses and movement to the intellectual, analytic function of the brain. This is as true at the couch as at a musical instrument. If we view behavior as an accretion of habits practiced over long periods of time, incorporating newly acquired behaviors demands practice. We live what we practice, not necessarily what we preach.

Breathing is the mechanism that binds everything together. Besides keeping us alive, it also allows us to slow down, release tension, pay attention, listen, become grounded, be present. Music, like breathing, is rooted in the body. It is therefore as dependent on getting oxygen as the body is. Without breathing there is no life; without breathing there is no music.

When we look at ancient Western concepts associated with the breath, we glimpse how encoded it is in the cosmic worldview. Breath, *pneuma*, has been associated from the time of the Greeks with the soul, *psyche*; with spirit, *anima* (from the Latin); with the divine; and with inspiration—literally, the breathing in of the divine. Indeed, according to sociologist Dr. Susan Phillips, contained within the Biblical commandment to keep the Sabbath is the exhortation to stop, breathe and notice.[21] Yet, in the religious fervor of keeping busy to which our modern society subscribes, we tend to neglect the sanctity of that breathing which connects us to the universe, to ourselves and to that spark of divinity—however we conceptualize that spark. When practiced at all, taking time is often rationalized in terms of needing rest to recharge our batteries and return to normal activity. The biological imperative to breathe that keeps us alive also keeps us connected to our world. Connection is breathing's partner.

The poet Stanley Burnshaw succinctly sums up that concept by writing: "For the mind when free to respond cannot help doing two things to whatever confronts it: it connects and it animates."[22] This quote is taken from his description of the mind's process in understanding poetry. I read it as illustrating the mind's recognition of the inherent value of whatever confronts it, with an implicit sense of the interrelationship of all things. As soon as there is more than one person, more than one note, more than one object, there is an implied connection.

In music, meaningful connections inhere between notes, phrases, sections, and movements. In fact, music must flow organically from the silence out of which it emerges. Egon Petri, considered one of the great pianists of the twentieth century, proclaimed that "continuity of movement is one of my obsessions."[23] The natural flow required in music is reflected in life when we are free to connect and respond to the present moment. As in music, the freedom to respond implies being in the present moment even as we are simultaneously connected to the moments before and after.

Breathing easily is invaluable in the process of self-discovery, whether as a musician or as a fully developed person. Learning to calm oneself and remain alert to one's environment is an exercise I often use in my practices. For most people it is liberating. Liza, a violist, surprised both herself and me after I led her through the Automatic Relax Response. When she opened her eyes and reconnected to the room we were in, she excitedly exclaimed: "Oh, my God! I never realized I could be both *calm and alert*, and *calm and active*. I always thought I had to keep my eyes closed, and sort of meditate when I got anxious. But then I couldn't do that while playing."

Though breathing fully is vital and liberating, it can also open up space for demons, or anxiety-producing energy, to emerge. When that happens, movement can aid in partially dispelling the demonic energy, making it easier eventually to confront and understand it. But it cannot be overemphasized that patience and time must be honored, for those demons too often grow out of the rubble of heart-wrenching stories.

I am reminded of Jenny, whose breathing was quick and shallow; she played the piano with wrists high, fingers feathering the keys. She gave me the impression she might float away at any moment.

"It scares me to be grounded," Jenny anxiously admitted, after trying to breathe calmly. "I'm still afraid of getting caught if I sit in my body. This way I'm safer—I can fly away if I need to." Eventually, Jenny recounted her early abuse. Like other abused children, Jenny had held her breath during her ordeal and floated above her body in dissociation. Since breathing had provoked fear, I asked her to slowly walk with me instead. After a bit, I wondered out loud if she could stop and try taking a small breath.

Softly she responded: "This is scary. I'm always waiting to feel like I'll fly away." We continued, and I assured her there was no hurry.

"It's still a bit panicky, but not like before. I keep wondering if I'm going to be punished for this." The fear of punishment frequently accompanies abused victims who have been warned against revealing their abuse. Jenny and I walked and walked with momentary breathing stops, until Jenny could stand still *and* more fully breathe at the same time.

Jenny courageously worked with me for a year to alleviate her fears of playing, and we moved often and readily between the emotional-couch work and music at the piano. Describing disturbing memories agitated her, and if she looked at me for help I would model easy breathing, letting soft sighs escape so she could hear them. In the middle of a Chopin Nocturne, Jenny stopped playing and looked at me. She was barely breathing. I asked her if she wanted to talk, but she shook her head "no."

"I want to breathe. Help me." I quickly moved toward her, then I heard her say, "I'd rather breathe than disappear."

What had happened while she played?

It was the sudden realization that her breathing was allowing her to truly hear herself for the first time, and it momentarily derailed her. Jenny's impulse was to stop breathing and "disappear myself." But instead, she decided to choose breathing and playing. It was an emotional moment for me as well, watching her battle the old tidal wave that could have carried her away.

The desire to float away, so thoroughly embedded from such a young age, was never completely abolished for Jenny. But she was learning to manage it.

Modeling and rehearsing new behaviors can be vital tools for both couch and piano work. *Practicing* and *rehearsing* are the buzzwords in the music studio, and teachers constantly model and shape students' musical conceptions. At the couch, modeling and practicing can be equally powerful tools, as we saw when Jenny needed help regaining equilibrium by watching and hearing me breathe. Breathing fully was a skill she had only recently acquired; it had not been practiced enough to become automatic. It would need more rehearsing.

Working with people who have internalized toxic psychic assaults taught me how such an experience can clog the sensory system. You will read (in chapter 5, "The Stories and Minds of Ariah") that the first thing Ariah said to me was, "I can't hear the music when I close my eyes." It can be a monumental feat in such a case, to learn how to open one's senses, continue to breathe and not become anxious. Modeling and practice enhance the learning.

The Body Is a Brain That Moves

Movement, whether it be walking, as Jenny did, or dancing, or even making random movements, can be the most direct, natural and simple means of examining an issue. Rodrigo consulted me about his recent performance for which he had conscientiously prepared. His playing was disappointing and he couldn't explain why. We searched together for possible answers, but to no avail. Then I asked him to symbolically retrace his steps from the moment he decided to perform to the moment of performing, by walking slowly from one end of the room to the other. If he thought of or sensed anything that interfered with his natural walk, he would stop and we'd talk. He started walking, and then suddenly he stopped.

"It was when I was asked to play at this particular function," he declared. "I didn't want to, I knew it was a mistake, but a friend asked so I let myself get talked into it and I didn't have a good reason not to play. I can feel even now how I got pulled off my walk, so to speak. It just felt wrong." He stood in one spot thinking for several long moments.

"I need to stay in touch with myself more, connected to here"—he pointed to his gut. "I think I'll have to practice what we just did, at home. It feels right. I feel *me*-ish," he said with a grin.

When I myself face a challenging, anxiety-producing event, I often get perspective from a dance I created for myself. It begins with three distinct stances or poses that I take with my body. One represents my life before the event, one represents me during the event and one my life after. Then I connect the stances with fluid, continual motion in hopes of nestling that discrete event into the larger context of my life, rather than letting it stick out as a distinct, awkward moment.

In large workshops where movement is limited, I ask participants to picture a problem they are working on, and to breathe and animate the problem into a concrete form. Then they sit back and engage in their own drama as they watch the internal "movie" of the problem. At one workshop with the staff of a hospital's physical therapy department, a nurse described needing to get along with a doctor she worked with but didn't like. When she closed her eyes, she saw the two of them stiffly passing each other in the corridor. But as she continued to breathe, they caught each other's eye in passing, and then incredulously turned into horses galloping freely in a field.

She came back from her gambol with a different sense of her colleague, less frozen in animosity, more fluid in possibilities. She indeed brought to life Burnshaw's statement, previously quoted, that a free mind connects and animates whatever confronts it.

While writing this chapter, I confronted frequent periods of hesitation. "So why don't you do this exercise?" I asked myself. Okay. I picture myself at my computer, writing. "I can't do this," I say to my computer. The computer gets very testy with me. "Why don't you read what you write? Look at the opening quote. Who said your struggle should be *easy*?" My own computer reflects back that I should practice what I preach. "You can't always get things easily. You have to work hard, like other people do, without whining. Tsk-tsk, Margret. Get on with it."

(I just took a break and practiced my three-stance dance. A little less angst. Might have to repeat many times!)

Moving may be a powerful mediator, but it can also create problems when uninvited. In the midst of a performance I gave many years ago, one of my legs started twitching, completely throwing off my concentration. I couldn't stop the shaking and have no idea how I managed to finish performing. Thinking it was a one-time nerve thing, I forgot about it. But after it repeated itself the next time I performed, I took the Zen approach and incorporated the shaking into my practice. I shook one leg, then the other. Then both. I made a game of it, shaking in time with the music, then shaking in different rhythms. My legs never twitched in performance again. Movement counteracting movement!

From there I applied the same technique to other unwanted body expressions. In anxious moments, hands can shake, the heart speed up, the mouth go dry. Sometimes, noses run (most embarrassing). Going directly into the area of interference instead of trying to stop it can prove the most effective means of management, much like the counterintuitive driving maneuver of turning the wheel of a car in the direction it is skidding so as not to create conflicting momentum. Like "dancing with the bull." That means, when the heart starts beating crazily during a performance, consciously going right to that area and letting the music come from the beating heart. Most of us are perverse *(and stubborn)* enough that as soon as we get permission to do something forbidden, it loses its power.

Sensory Awareness

We learn through our senses—hearing, seeing, feeling, smelling and tasting—and what we experience gets translated by our brain. The more senses involved in learning, the stronger the potential for learning and remembering. Our cognitive ability helps us make judgments and discern the best course to follow. But the brain also acts as a nonjudgmental repository for accumulated repetition. With enough repetition, synaptic connections are made in the brain, whether they serve us or not. That is why it is often difficult to rid ourselves of habits no longer desirable. Adding the senses to the process reinforces the intellect. And, knowing exactly what you wish to learn is the first step in the process. As master piano teacher Alexander Libermann admonished: "Practice doesn't make perfect; it makes permanent."[24]

Learning is enhanced by opening visual, auditory and kinesthetic channels. In learning music, visual awareness includes the written page, how the hands look when playing correctly, and the geography of the instrument as you play correctly. Kinesthetic awareness refers to the feeling of your hands as they play accurately, as well as to the internal kinesthetic—or feeling—that each part of the music elicits. Auditory awareness, most importantly, consists of the sound of the music, to which I add speaking out loud while learning, and then hearing the echo of that voice when it has been internalized.

Listening and paying attention are essential in every aspect of our lives. Despite the fact that, in our frenetic, technology-dominated world, listening and paying attention are endangered attributes, they are the glue of true relationships: between ourselves and our art; between friends; among family; with all our surroundings.

At the couch, clinicians watch for visual cues and pay attention to their own internal feelings, or countertransference. They listen not only to the words spoken, but also for those unsaid, to tone of voice and to silence as well. For, like the many shades of a color and the many intonations of speech, there are multiple meanings to silence just as there are multiple meanings to the silences of musical rests.

People with dissociative behavior often vacate the present when it becomes unbearable to remain. Reconnecting through their senses often helps return them to the present. When I felt one such client mentally drifting away from our session as she looked out the window, I followed her gaze and softly commented. "I hear birds. They're talking a lot, aren't they? Do you see any? Put your hands beside you on the couch and feel the softness of the material. Feel the connection between your fingers and the fabric." Slowly, my voice, her awareness of her surroundings and my repeated suggestion that she was safe helped bring her focus back. Eventually we made guidelines for her to bring herself back when, feeling alone and afraid, she'd disappear. And we practiced those guidelines together a great deal.

Cultivating these sensory connections stimulates our vitality. Though it may seem paradoxical, connecting with silence enriches, as well. Connecting with silence is akin to taking time to just *be*—whether during the Sabbath or any day. And what a challenge that is for most of us! We are not programmed for stillness. Faced with silence, we rush to fill the space with talking—out loud or to ourselves. Mindfulness is one antidote for mindless filling of space. My version of it—and how I connect to myself and to the present—is called Sitting-in-the-Release.

Sitting-in-the-Release: Replacing Apprehension with Composure

Sitting-in-the-Release (see Section IV, Terms & Exercises) not only is a grounding exercise, but also serves as an underlying mechanism for changing behavior. It combines breathing to your internal cue, becoming calm, connecting to the environment by opening sensory channels and remaining in that quiet space for a few moments.

Breathing, watching, listening, feeling—these make up a prescription for intervention when one wishes to exchange an undesirable habit for more productive behavior. Examples of such behavior? Uh-Oh moments: those spots in music that have become associated with mental apprehension and physical tension; or the moment in an argument that regularly goes awry between two people. Sitting-in-the-Release brings stillness and creates space for making desired choices. Coming out of this calm/alert state, your body and mind are able to replace an old response with a new one. Then it is time for practicing the new behavior.

In our search for wholeness, we need to embrace many small steps on the way. I am reminded of a delightful quote from master piano teacher Egon Petri: "I sometimes say to the music, 'Excuse me, Madame. Wait in the next room while I take this passage out and work on it.'"[25]

Small steps, patience, awareness—these were beautifully realized in the following dream, related to me by a musician while we sat at the couch:

> *I dreamed I was walking in what was supposed to be a garden. At first the earth looked all brown and barren and I felt cold and scared. My first instinct was to become immobilized with fear like I usually do when frightened or worried. But then I heard your voice calming me. I said to myself, "Breathe. This is your garden. Look around you. Pay attention." I stood still, breathed, and then calmly I looked down. There I saw tiny green shoots just pushing their way up through the earth. I started to cry. And as I felt my feet planted like sprouts in that spot in the garden, with tears falling as if watering the spot, I realized what I sought was right in front of me: the spiritual connection I had been seeking for so long was there in my garden.*

Where the Truth Lives: De-glitchifying

We have been speaking of moments in life and music that need reevaluating and changing. I call those moments "Glitches": the Uh-Oh spots in our music; the spot of derailment from our own purpose; the place where the fighting begins. Despite recognizing the need to change, we often continue putting off dealing with—or de-glitchifying—them. Perhaps the unconscious knowledge that there may be demons lurking within keeps us from probing. And though we may experience demons and glitches differently, they both invite us to delve, confront, learn, grow. Every part of the de-glitchifying process—from identifying to analyzing and dissecting the exact spot, to incorporating the necessary changes—testifies to our commitment to take ourselves seriously. As one student told me after years of habitually glossing over musical mistakes, as well as accepting unhappy relationships in her life, "I am finally willing to go to where the truth is. For me that means when I practice I want to know exactly what needs work. No more fudging. In life I don't want to say, 'It doesn't matter' anymore. It matters."

I watch a pianist make a quick, big leap from one chord to the next. And miss the notes. The student's hands land in the general area of the chord, then search for the notes. "Slow down," I say. "Eyeball the chord you're going to and go directly. Don't hover, looking for a landing spot."

My student looks up with a knowing smile. "I guess it helps to know where you're going. I've been guessing, just happy to get to the general vicinity." It matters, I agree, in learning music, to know where you're going.

In writing this book, I am continually reminded that everything in my life—relationships, students and clients, passages and pieces of music—helps illuminate the meaning for me of my own life; each endeavor is a kernel of the person I was meant to be. Even if I'm not truthful to myself one hundred percent of the time, I feel a commitment to myself to go where my truth lies. In the case studies that follow, you will witness how others have grappled in their searches for their own truth; how they faced their demons and confronted the challenge of de-glitchifying; how they slowed down to make space for discovering what they need in order to fully inhabit themselves. Seeking takes *courage*, a word that shares its Latin root with words for *heart*. The reward for seeking, for baring one's soul, is connecting to one's heart and saying, *Oh, yes. This is where I belong. I'm home.*

SECTION II

CASE STUDIES

THREE

CELESTE - THE DRAGON AND DEBUSSY

Teach yourself to see through the back of your neck, the crown of your head, your temple and even your footprints.
— Matiushin, early-twentieth-century Soviet painter

Celeste, who had the dream of a couch by the piano, walked into our final session with a light step and comfortably settled back in the cushiony chair. She wore a flattering, close-fitting dress and her poise and confidence were reassuring. She began by referring to the book she was reading, *The Piano Tuner.* I asked what brought that to mind.

"I was just thinking how the man in the book knows how he feels by thinking of a particular piece of music."

"What piece are *you* feeling, Celeste, at this moment?"

It was an apt question, for that moment held the weight of many feelings. We had worked together for six years, grappling with Celeste's lifelong torments that took shape as devouring dragons, taunting demons. We had confronted the anguish that froze her with fear at the piano, her hypochondria and her early abuse. We had sat together at the piano and at the couch as she alternated between viewing me as another agent of torment in her life and as an agent of freedom. She had played, cried and fallen apart. Now I wondered, as Celeste took time and pondered the question: What piece was she feeling?

"'*Clair de Lune*' . . . it starts out misty, warm, then it becomes very emotional.

At the end. . . . Well, it doesn't really end, it gets soft, goes on. . . . It feels like it continues after the ending."

We both smiled. Her description of the dreamy, coloristic piece by Debussy captured precisely what the moment held: a termination that contained the thematic strands that would lead her into her future; no fanfare—simply going on with her life. For Celeste, after experiencing the *Sturm und Drang* of many sessions with me, the soft continuity she described was a loud testament to her strength and determination.

Celeste and I had been introduced at a concert by a mutual friend saying we were both pianists. The friend casually mentioned that I also work with emotional issues of performers. Celeste had moved with her husband and two daughters from a small Midwestern town and was thrilled to be in a cultured urban environment. She looked to be in her forties; she was very attractive, tall, lean, with short-cropped blond hair. She seemed competent, self-assured and friendly.

It was three years later that she called me to ask about my work and to set up an appointment. When she first came to see me, I thought she'd sent a scared, anxious, younger twin. She hesitantly entered my studio, meekly asked if it was okay for us to sit on the chairs away from the piano and then perched on the edge of her chair the entire session.

"It's nice to see you, Celeste. I sense it's been a difficult decision to come here." She flashed a nervous but warm smile in agreement.

"It's taken a long time to get the nerve to call," she replied. "And I don't even know what to say now that I'm here."

I in turn smiled in what I hoped appeared an understanding and friendly response. After some moments of silence, I suggested she tell me a little about herself. Haltingly, eyes downcast, she related her musical history.

Celeste had been taking piano lessons without interruption since she was a child. For the last twenty years she had studied with Madame Linsky, a teacher of renown who taught in the music school in the large city close to Celeste's town. She became a figure of enormous influence over Celeste. In fact, Celeste was still going back once a month to see this teacher, who was now in her seventies. With great hesitation, Celeste said it might be time to change teachers despite her continued devotion and gratitude toward "Madame," as she called her. As I listened to

Celeste, I heard hints of an emotionally thick student/teacher relationship extending well beyond the music studio. Silently I listened to this adult, trembling like a child, relate how she forced herself to take the plunge to see me.

"After all these years of studying, I can barely sit down and play a piece through for myself, and certainly not if anyone is around. Oh," she said with a radiant smile, "but I *do* play for the children in the kindergarten class I volunteer in—that's something I love to do, and it's easy. I love watching them as they move to the music; they're so free." Then she added, "Like I'd like to be.

"I even teach piano at home to a few of them; their moms asked me to, after watching what I do in the classroom. But it's just for fun. The time with the kids is the freest I get." Then, suddenly more somber: "I'd like to feel that way when I play. Well, in fact, I'd like to feel that way in my life in general."

When it was time to end our session, Celeste asked if she could return. She liked the idea of exploring ways to find more freedom. While we discussed scheduling, she timidly remarked that she preferred mornings. "Eight would be perfect," she said.

A late-night person myself, I inwardly groaned at this suggestion. But it was evident that Celeste had a terrible time asking for anything for herself; even as I was checking my schedule she was saying, "But of course, if that's not good for you. . . ."

My first act needed to honor her request; later I would figure out how to reconfigure my sleep schedule the night before our appointment. I agreed: 8 a.m. it would be. We said goodbye. Celeste jumped up and left as if freed from imprisonment.

Nourishment: To Eat or Not

Early on, Celeste reported a dream. She was standing in front of a house that resembled mine. She saw three linen-draped tables in the window, and realized it was an elegant restaurant. Madame Linsky, her previous piano teacher, resided in the back. Celeste stood there wondering if she could make a reservation.

Like a Haiku poem of seventeen syllables, this little gem of a dream, the first reported in our work together, encapsulated an important theme: the need for nourishment and the doubt of attaining it. That theme would accompany us throughout our work. Would Celeste be stuck in old, cloistered ways that no longer fed her? Or would she be free to dine well in a light-filled environment? Could she walk through the front door into the house that resembled mine to attain the freedom she sought?

I wondered what lessons were like with Madame Linsky.

"It was like walking into a different world, a world apart. I came for her blessing. Any suggestion, however mild, felt like a punishment, a judgment from on high. I couldn't bear to fail her. With Madame I was a different person. . . . I wasn't me."

"Who were you?"

Her answer was revealing. "She was someone from another place—unreal, sacred to me . . ."

I interrupted her. "Celeste, I asked who *you* were."

"Oh. I didn't hear." Pause, thinking. "I was not me. It was as if I was a pretend person. It didn't matter whether I played well or not, I felt like I was in a sacred environment." Celeste thought a moment before continuing. "She didn't have any children—perhaps I was a surrogate daughter?"

I was struggling to understand the complicated threads that connected Celeste to Madame Linsky. Clearly, the young student felt awe in her teacher's presence and needed her blessing, her love, her acceptance. Any indication, no matter how tiny, of not being worthy, of feeling criticized, was experienced as a narcissistic blow, a blow to her entire self. And, did she also intuit in her teacher an underlying need for that most fundamental of emotional connections: that between mother and daughter? Did they both need that?

"What about your connection with your own mother?" I asked gently.

Sadness descended as Celeste looked away. "Mostly, I felt alone as a child. If I fell or hurt myself I'd get a quick hug. Otherwise, I pretty much took care of myself. Actually, I often had to take care of my older twin brothers too, who constantly got in trouble. My mom was so wrapped up in herself." I barely caught the flickering of emotion that crossed her countenance. A mixture of anger and resignation? "And now of course she's older and I have to look out for her, too."

Celeste, an emotionally deprived child, had found a surrogate mother in Madame who could lavish the attention on her that every child craves. On the positive side of this equation was the acceptance and love she received through this attachment and its constancy. But the equation was balanced with the claustrophobic quality of the relationship and Madame Linsky's need for her student/

daughter's exclusive allegiance. Actual musical progress was undoubtedly second-ary to the emotional bonds cemented through the relationship.

During the first few months of our work, Celeste and I sat at the keyboard most of the time, but so many nonmusical issues came up that we did a lot of "couch" work there, as well. There was so much anxiety attached both to her daily life and to being in the studio with me that I knew additional measures were essential. I introduced her to my breathing exercise—already discussed—that steadies mind and body while allowing for remaining connected to one's surroundings. I sug-gested that Celeste practice it a few minutes daily away from the piano until it became an Automatic Relax Response. We then discussed ways that she could use the exercise to calm herself throughout the day.

When Celeste first ventured to play for me, it was with a tight, tiny, "please-don't-hear-me" sound, so we went through the steps aimed at playing with ease and making a bigger sound. Celeste dutifully followed the steps of calming herself and letting weight drop from shoulder to arms. She lifted her arms above the key-board and released them, her hands falling onto the piano with a free fall, making a resounding crash. The sound filled the room. Silently I cheered, for the purpose of the exercise is to experience the power of arm weight when allowed to fall natu-rally. It's the same feeling as the natural swinging of our arms as we walk.

At the moment of impact, however, Celeste visibly recoiled, eyes clearly fear-ful. I immediately moved toward her in a gesture of support. In answer to my raised eyebrows, she stammered, "That's very scary." Silence. "If I play loud, someone might hear me." More moments of silence as I waited to see if she would expand on her statement. She didn't.

"Like who?" I asked sympathetically.

Nervously, with eyes flitting: "Well, maybe my mom. She'd be mad if I dis-turbed her." And, once disturbed, her mom might come tearing into the room in an uncontrollable rage, reducing Celeste to a tiny, trembling child. "Please, let's not talk about that now," she begged.

I sat back in my chair and assumed a relaxed stance. Eventually we would address issues surrounding "big sound" and "ease," not to mention "mom." But not today. Celeste had clearly indicated that we needed to take a step back. As if to clear the air, she quickly reported experiencing more ease at home at the piano.

"That's great," I said, noting the change into a less-anxiety-producing atmosphere. It prompted me to follow with an observation.

"I wonder if you are aware that you sit slightly to the right of center at the keyboard, and close to the edge . . ."

Celeste interrupted before I ended my sentence, moving even closer to the edge. "I always sit like that. Like at dinner . . . it keeps me from being really present." Her self-awareness spurred me to continue.

"Tell me about dinner. Better yet, draw me a diagram." She drew the seating arrangement for her family: husband and two daughters. Her own chair was squeezed next to the wall, body poised to jump up, ready to serve.

"Your music homework for this week," I said slyly, "is to change one little thing at dinner . . ."

Celeste quickly interrupted: "I'll pull out my chair from the wall so I have more space."

I realized when she left that she had led us directly into the theme of her restaurant dream: nourishment, and how to attain it.

Dinnertime was as good a place as any to start helping her become aware of her taut, anxiety-fraught existence. As she began learning the physical means of releasing excess tension, whether at dinner or at the piano, her relationship with her body came to the forefront. At one lesson she happily reported having practiced with ease, left hand alone, then immediately added, "But my elbow hurt."

I waited for her to continue. She looked at me as if pondering whether to trust me, then timidly referred to having serious somatic fears.

"Such as?" I wondered.

"I'm afraid I have multiple sclerosis . . . or ovarian cancer."

"Have you asked your doctor about that?"

"Yes. My regular tests are normal and I'm past the age where people usually get M.S. But of course there are exceptions. . . ." She looked sheepish saying this, looking to me for what response I couldn't tell.

I took a chance with a humorous retort. "Oh. So you're a hypochondriac. Why didn't you say so?" She nodded and laughed.

"What does your doctor say?"

"To see a therapist." She paused. "That's what they told my mom when I was young. Because I threw up so much."

Over the next few months I continued learning about Celeste's emotionally lonely childhood. When she fell, she got a quick hug and a Band-Aid. If she felt sad or just needed a hug, she was told not to be silly. When either of the twin brothers got angry and hit her, she was blamed and the brother got a treat, or so she remembered. When she herself showed the slightest sign of noncompliance, her mother lost control, screaming and throwing dishes. A neighbor once called the police. Despite the strained relationship with her siblings, she felt abandoned and isolated when they left home—an escape they made as early as they could.

As a pretty child with long blond hair, she had attracted sexualized attention from an uncle and some of her young friends' fathers. I realized then that I had only seen her dressed in loose-fitting clothing, a mode of dress often pursued by women whose body had attracted unwanted attention. Haltingly, she described the many memories of being bounced on friendly men's laps, their hands wandering up her legs. She denied that they raped her, and though I wondered whether she had repressed memories of such activities, memories that could further explain her episodes of throwing up, I did not press her. If she needed to, she would retrieve those memories herself.

Slowly, Celeste began regarding my studio as a haven where she could say anything without fear of judgment. She also allowed herself to think out loud, often surprising herself. Almost apologetically, but with subdued exuberance, Celeste admitted:

"I want to teach piano full time to children, not just for fun but like a professional. I would like to quit volunteering at the kindergarten and plunge into teaching. But I can't leave my volunteering for at least two years."

"Why not? It's March now. With planning, you could leave this fall."

Almost automatically, she exclaimed, "Oh, I couldn't. They'd need to find other parents to replace me."

"If you give notice now, they have plenty of time. There's even time for you to help initiate the new volunteers." I was undoubtedly pushing the envelope with this suggestion, but she later revealed that it had been a pivotal moment.

Celeste struggled, over the next months, to take small steps out of her self-imprisonment. She worked to carve out time for herself at the piano and to disengage from being on call 24/7 to her family and everyone else. She became clearer about her goals and the steps needed to achieve them, such as telling her family the times she'd be practicing and not be available. She allowed herself an occasional lunch with friends.

Celeste began identifying her many physical pains as storage areas for her generalized angst. As we continued our work, feelings were emerging that, like hungry bears after winter, were coming out of hibernation with a vengeance. One hour per week together seemed inadequate to contain and address the full panoply of issues *and* to retrain her musically. Though we never shied away from addressing and incorporating whatever issues came up, my instinct told me she should be in a fully therapeutic environment outside our work, as well. I was preparing to open this discussion with her the next time I saw her, when she announced she had decided to go into therapy and asked for a recommendation, which I gladly provided.

At the same time, she told me she'd given notice to the school and wouldn't be returning in the fall. Even as teachers, students and parents begged her to stay, she weathered their disappointment and held her ground. She told me that the question I had posited about postponing this decision had echoed in her mind and made her question herself about putting other people's needs before her own. By the fall of the following year, her piano studio was growing.

Haven and Hell

Though my studio had increasingly become Celeste's safe refuge, it would abruptly morph into an arena of persecution when she stepped away from "couch" work and toward playing the piano. As long as we faced each other discussing teacher–studio issues like dealing with parents, her studio policy or teaching Baroque style, she was comfortable. But when she faced playing the piano, she turned into a young child. In her eyes I became the judgmental, punitive teacher, waiting to "call her out" for making mistakes. She slipped into a frozen mental state, unable to absorb anything related to her playing that I told her.

Sitting beside Celeste, I watched how she'd become mentally inaccessible, her body stiff and her face and eyes drained of emotion. She wasn't experiencing full-blown dissociative states; she responded to suggestions to walk around the room and could answer questions about her feelings. But, sitting as a student at the keyboard, she was clearly frightened enough to emotionally separate out a part of herself.

For the next two years, we worked between the couch and the piano. It was clear that Celeste needed relief from her disabling anxiety. Perhaps, I thought, if we revisited the exercises that had once benefitted her, they could now lead us into deeper territory and reinforce her increasing self-awareness.

As Celeste turned once again to becoming aware of her breathing and how it affected the release of tension from her shoulders, she made a profound discovery: There was an important piece missing from her life—an awareness of her body. Celeste was becoming conscious of how little she inhabited all her body parts, other than to experience pain. Thus, as she continued to release tension, she experienced her body in the way most familiar to her: with pain. After one session spent on finding ease in her hands, she complained of lower back pain. There was, however, a bright side to it: "At least I *have* a lower back here. At home I don't feel my back at all."

Here I was again, both surprised and chagrined. I wanted to have ready-made answers for whatever arose in my studio, yet here was someone for whom releasing tension brought pain. I breathed to my own internal cue and reminded myself to remain calm and fluid in outlook as I watched her body slowly coming back to life after years of being blocked off from her conscious experience of it. It literally jerked and twitched as it woke up. We'd laugh as Celeste wiggled on the bench, unable to find a comfortable position, and as she proudly pointed out, "I'm not doing my dying thing. I'm not panicking and running to the doctor."

That, we agreed, was progress.

Even as Celeste became adept at decreasing physical tension, she had difficulty in accessing that ease at the piano. As we've discussed previously, working hard is the sine qua non of accomplishing goals in our society, inculcated as we are to believe that hard work is virtue, ease akin to laziness (see Section III: Metaphors). Accomplishment without pain, struggling or suffering can provoke a crisis of faith and self-worth.

Celeste was quick to identify an apt analogy for herself: cleaning. "When I scrub toilets," she told me, "I do it till they shine. I vacuum to within an inch of my life." And she proceeded to dramatize how every fiber of her being went into those activities, brows furrowed and eyes focused on scrubbing with clenched hands. When I tried mirroring how her body looked, we both broke into laughter.

At the piano, her biggest hurdle was changing her mind-set from thinking that taking time during practice, breathing and finding ease meant she was lazy, even worthless. As with many other students, it practically entailed a religious conversion to discover that hard work did not necessarily involve tension, speed and breathlessness. Importantly, Celeste could now notice when the scrubbing response replaced the calming response, even though she couldn't yet change it at will.

Breakdown/Breakthrough

Summer arrived and Celeste declared that she was ready to begin lessons in earnest, stating, "I want to play without fear. And I want to start with Bach." Hearing those declarations, I put on my teacher's hat to decide where to begin. Over the last few years, I had heard Celeste play snippets of pieces, but they had quickly veered us onto emotional tracks. Therefore, I did not yet have an accurate view of her pianistic capabilities. We spent several frustrating months with a Bach French Suite, considered of intermediate difficulty. Celeste came back week after week, like a young child, unable to learn even simple passages or to retain what we'd gone over at previous lessons.

Mistakes of notes and timing continued; there was little sense of voicing or phrasing, essential aspects of musical interpretation. I was plagued by my own mental diatribe based on disbelief and exasperation. I caught myself thinking: *What's wrong with you? Why can't you count? How can you make so many mistakes? What happened to all those years of lessons?* In retrospect, I know her unconscious needed to play out this old dynamic as a pull toward my understanding her better. But, clueless when it happened, I would buckle down to dissect small sections of the pieces and explore methods of learning and memorizing.

Six months after we began "lessons in earnest," Celeste was playing a Chopin Prelude and I noticed that, while her hands appeared to be playing with ease and her sound was rich and solid—healthy signs of progress—she retained the demeanor of a young child, shoulders slightly slumped, face taut. I gently noted the dichotomy to her. She put her head on top of the piano and covered her head with her arms.

"There's still a part of me that's very afraid of making big sounds."

"But what part of you made that solid sound just now?"

"Well, just everyday me."

Her matter-of-fact response, that it was her everyday self that made the solid sound, excited me. I interpreted that as a pull toward an authentic self. I asked her to step into the center of the room and first take the stance of her fearful self and then her "everyday" self, and vocalize the experience. She reported going from "small, scared" to "big, free." But "big, free" frightened her, and she recoiled once again into her "small, scared" stance. She blurted out, "That really hit," and pointed to her stomach. When I asked what she was pointing to, she responded, "Loneliness, sadness; it feels like when I was four."

As we were presently working within the context of a piano lesson, I invited her to direct her intense emotion back at the piano. I asked: "Do you wish to play something *for*—or perhaps *with*—your four-year-old self?"

"With." She instantly responded. She played while providing a running commentary. "Am I going crazy—isn't this insane talking to your four-year-old self? Well, I wasn't only sad then, I danced a lot too, to my father's records. . . . I had a lot of joy and movement then. . . . Am I crazy?"

I assured her she wasn't crazy and that it would be great if she could let herself retrieve her four-year-old energy from the time when she danced with joy.

The following week, Celeste came in disoriented. She was simultaneously questioning her own sanity while continuing dialogues with the part of herself that had emerged in the previous lesson. In addition, during a particularly moving discussion with her husband, she confessed to him: "I found my young child and I've been talking to her." And her husband, his surprised wife told me, "Completely got it!" Maybe she wasn't going crazy after all.

All this set the stage for what occurred in the weeks that followed. Celeste would arrive anxious to play, but again and again the simple piece unraveled under her fingers. As she played, she continually commented on what was happening: "I played that wrong"; "I can't seem to get this"; "I'm not sure about the counting."

Once again, my frustration mounted as I listened to her tone of voice—that of a plaintive child—and watched what appeared to be willful incompetence. I felt as if she were tugging at me, forcing me to yell at her and criticize her. I was having a visceral reaction to her entrenched, little-girl behavior until I finally understood at last: Celeste, in her unconscious wisdom, was replaying a dynamic pattern in her life with me. We would need to unravel its meaning together.

I put my hand on her arm. "Let's stop a moment, shall we? I'm going to tell you something that's happening with me now that I'd like to explore with you." She looked puzzled, even expectant. I took a few moments to gather my thoughts.

"I'm getting a *very* strong feeling that you are pulling for me to get angry with you, to say punitive things. Does this sound . . ."

The dam burst open. Celeste threw herself off the piano bench and walked in a frenzy, circling the room. She came back and stood, shaking, by the side of the piano, holding it for support.

"Yes, yes . . . that's it . . ." Tears interfered with her words. "I can't stop myself. It's what I've always done. I've always felt like I'd never be able to play anything well, always needing my teacher to tell me what to do, I couldn't sustain it myself. I just want to be . . ." She tripped on her words.

"Taken care of?" I asked.

"Yes. I don't know how to do this on my own."

"What do you think would happen if you were to play as you'd like?"

"Responsibility. But not just that: fear. Fear that I'd find out I really can't play, and then I'd also have to give up teaching. I can't get beyond feeling like a child at lessons. Every criticism, which means *anything* said to me about my playing, is a judgment against me," she cried out, shoulders slumping. She looked like a Raggedy Ann doll with its insides removed.

"Where are you physically aware of this conflict?"

She pointed immediately to her stomach and almost doubled over. "I'm always afraid I'm going to vomit." She was crouching now in a ball on the floor. Instinctively I crouched down beside her.

My own words tumbled out even before I thought them. "How does it sound to you if we were to create a new scenario for your piano lessons? If we let go of all traditional expectations that you prepare for them, and see what you want when you get here? We'll create an entirely novel concept of piano lessons."

She burst into tears. "I feel like a valve has just been opened—inside, it feels like a huge release. Sometimes at these lessons, the tiniest word of kindness would reverberate throughout my body." After a moment: "But what kind of lessons would they be? What would people think?"

I stopped myself from smiling at her automatic response to worry about the opinion of others. "Our goal is for *you* to get music back for *yourself*. Everything that occurs here furthers that goal. It doesn't matter how it might look to anyone else."

"All I want is to become friends with the piano," she said, sighing deeply. I moved slightly away as she drew herself together, involved in my own thoughts about what I'd proposed. I wondered whether taking away traditional structure and having permission to come to lessons without expectations might prove scary to Celeste. Even if her old lessons didn't provide her with musical sustenance, they did provide predictable stability and comfort. Now we were about to play with a new set of ground rules, aimed at freeing her. But would it?

As I was ruminating, Celeste volunteered her own ruminations. "I'm thinking about the freedom this will give me and how, sometimes at home, I'd find myself playing freely and then become dizzy and have to stop. I'd remember my mother screaming out of control when the sounds of the piano upset her and of my brother out of control on drugs." The freedom that Celeste momentarily grabbed for herself as a child had become synonymous with being "out of control" and needing containment. The containment grew stronger until it overtook exuberance.

"What will *now* help change how you feel about lessons?" I asked.

"I think I want to start from scratch. I just want to sit on a single note, for example on F, and wait for all the weight to drop."

"Why F?" I was curious.

She paused a moment, visualizing the treble clef. "Because it's the first note on a space."

I smiled. Space was indeed what Celeste needed now. In response to her having said she wanted to make friends with the piano, I called her attention to the chapter in my book *Passionate Practice* called "Creating a Partnership with Your Instrument." Using the exercises there would help her discover how to cultivate childlike curiosity, facilitating the path to making friends with the piano.

My Piano, Myself

When Celeste returned the following week, she immediately launched into her experience with the exercises, one of which is to walk all around the piano, feeling its multiple textures. "I was exploring the piano at home, touching it all over. . . . I realized that the bottom line for me is about slowing down, paying attention. I never thought those tasks could be so hard. Well, I never thought about them at all! I mean, it's like a recurrent dream of mine where I'm wearing layers, like a burka, over my eyes and I can't see.

"This week, I also did the exercise of drawing pictures of the piano. While I was drawing, I started becoming sensitive to the piano's personality and character-istics. It gave me a different sense of my world, like waking up and seeing for the first time. Even though it was exhilarating, it was also sad. What have I missed all this time by not seeing?"

We sat together in that poignant moment and I sensed Celeste's feeling of loss at not having been present in her own life. My hope was that she would recognize that her future could be different.

"What is it you don't want to see, Celeste?"

Too quickly she answered, "Me. My feelings."

Such an immediate response would be the top layer of responses.

"And what else?"

This time she paused before responding. "I don't want to *be* seen, either." I thought about her loose-fitting clothing. "If people saw me, they'd know I was an impostor, not really who they think I am. That I'm not a real musician."

"What constitutes a real musician?"

"Someone who went to the conservatory, speaks other languages, knows the repertoire."

"And a good teacher is . . ."

"Someone with patience, who has a natural knack for teaching, who takes each student on his own merit and can provide what that individual student needs."

I anticipated, from our chats about teaching, her answer to my next question. "And as a teacher, do you have those qualities?"

Looking straight at me, she said a simple: "Yes." We both seemed pleased at her straightforward answer, one that acknowledged her strength.

"Then you have what it naturally takes to be a good teacher. You can always fill gaps in your musical education. What do you imagine it would be like if you filled those gaps?"

"I'd feel at ease at the keyboard and freely demonstrate the pieces my students are working on."

"How can those goals be accomplished?" I asked, conjecturing to myself that she'd been thinking about such issues during the week, perhaps while making friends with her piano.

"I'm going to go through the *Mikrokosmos* [a set of progressive pieces in seven volumes by Béla Bartók] slowly . . . counting . . . bringing in questions to you without feeling ashamed that I don't know all the answers. And, I'm going to go through your book slowly, not like the last time, when I skimmed through at breakneck speed." After a pause, she added: "I'm grateful for the space to do that here. It feels right."

Bird on a Limb

The New Year was new in several ways. One of Celeste's first declarations of independence was canceling a lesson with me. As she'd never canceled a lesson before, she found it an act of liberation. She continued taking control of her musical life by devising a daily practice plan: It began with a soothing cup of tea, followed by slowly going through breathing, visualizing and energy-releasing exercises. She'd sight-read from the *Mikrokosmos*, then begin learning a Bach Invention, and, to finish off, revisit a beloved Mozart Sonata.

We worked on Baroque and Classical style, and on musical phrasing—the inflection that makes music intelligible as sentence and paragraph structures do in writing. We worked on her difficulty in counting rests at the ends of phrases and rushing from one phrase to the next. It was a mark of Celeste's emotional development that she could openly deal with her musical gaps, even as she struggled with shame for what she didn't know. During the day away from the piano, she practiced walking with freely swinging arms, breathing and even counting as she walked. She visualized herself at the piano just being her everyday self, playing without fear.

Celeste kept a journal by her piano at home and often related its contents to me. One week, she read to me about her four-year-old self's joining her while she practiced.

"I felt an internal shift as I played. One of those moments when I was just playing and not constantly harping at myself. . . . It felt wonderful. But then I caught myself feeling good and pulled away. I suddenly felt vulnerable—like a bird at the edge of a limb." The wonderful image of a bird sitting at the edge of a limb flew into my mind, and captured the ambivalence that young adults have when perched on the threshold of independence, wondering if they're ready. When I relayed that vision to Celeste, she nodded emphatic agreement and immediately brought that vision into the musical arena.

"That's exactly how I feel at the end of phrases—like in the Mozart Sonata. Afraid to just hang out there, at the edge of the limb, with the quarter-note rests, to leave the security of holding onto the piano and the sound—I need to hurry through, I feel so vulnerable."

Away from my studio, Celeste became more self-observant, noticing and talking about old patterns, beginning to let down her defenses. She noticed how she turned into the perfect young daughter when her parents visited, washing, cooking and care-taking. She reported her nervousness before lessons each week, thinking to herself: "What will Margret think? Is she going to tell me she won't teach me anymore?" Such observations may sound very prosaic to others—I mean, what son or daughter *doesn't* occasionally feel like a child again when parents are around? What music student *doesn't* worry about the teacher's response? For Celeste, being aware of such patterns and the extent to which they influenced her was an entirely new experience. Talking openly about them gave her the opportunity to evaluate and distinguish the patterns' most-toxic elements.

One day, I watched Celeste as I encouraged her to experiment with different phrasings for Bach's C-Major Invention. She became increasingly frustrated. Sensing her fear, I looked at her and realized she was "absent." She had mentally dissociated herself from the present, from her lesson, and had gone somewhere else. I looked directly at her. "Wait a moment, Celeste. What's happening?"

She snapped back. "I got afraid and left." I caught her eyes. Slowly the fearful expression written in her wide eyes and clenched jaw unfolded as we talked.

"What happened immediately before you 'left'?"

She gulped air. "I couldn't imitate what I heard you do. I got scared and left."

I nodded reassuringly, and placed my hand on her arm. "Can we find a way for you to stay present when you get afraid?"

She nodded, yes. There was silence. I looked at her expectantly—only to see *her* looking at *me* expectantly.

"*Ohhh*—you want *me* to find a way?" she said, and we both laughed. There was a shift in the air as she thought. "Hmm. I could say, 'Margret, I don't understand how this goes—can you show me again?'"

We nodded to each other in agreement. She continued, freely associating. "Sometimes it's a feeling of showing off when I get it right. Will I be punished? Or . . . it's about being seen, too."

I waited. Something important hovered in the air.

"When I was with my parents last week, they wanted me to play. I started to panic. It was just like when I was young and they kept telling me to play for their friends." She stopped. There was a long silence.

"What else comes up about being young, Celeste?"

She looked down. Her breathing was shallow and she seemed to go inside herself. "There was this time when these boys took me in a room and made me strip. They didn't do anything, just wanted to see, but it was awful . . . and there was also an uncle of mine who took me on his lap—I was cute with long, silky hair—and fondled me . . . inside me, too, with his hands . . ." She paused. "It hurt."

She was surprisingly present as she described these violations.

"How does talking about those incidents affect you?"

"Lonely. Very sad and lonely."

"Such times when you were an object for someone else's pleasure—to satisfy boys' curiosity, or male lust, or your parents' pride—you, Celeste, weren't being seen; only the part they wanted to see counted. Absenting yourself was self-preservation then." I paused. " I'm glad you talk about these things here."

"I feel very safe here. Once I'm here. I never told anyone about the boys." Moments passed. She sat quietly, as did I. I knew moments like these, full of conflicting sensations, could easily lead Celeste to mentally dissociate from the present, thereby getting "rid" of the feelings. I also knew she often deflected further talk at such moments. Wanting her to both stay present and not lose her feelings, I wondered aloud if she could use her feelings as a bridge to the piano.

"Can you play one phrase of the Bach, staying present no matter what? Never mind wrong notes or anything."

She turned to the music and with a great deal of presence played the first phrase. Then she precipitously got up, as she often did when she was unable to sustain playing unselfconsciously. I said nothing, wondering what she would do next.

Slowly she made her way back to the piano.

"Let me tell you how I view our time together, our *contract*," I said quietly. "The time here is yours, and you decide how you want to use it. Everything that happens here I consider relevant to your music, even when you don't play." She had calmed down by now and looked pensive.

"That's still such a strange notion," she responded. "I still feel it hasn't been a good lesson if I don't get punished—you know, scolded for not doing it right. At least I'm not afraid that I'll vomit anymore." She looked up with a smile. "I got over it and graduated to better fears." We laughed.

Then I heard her wistfully say, "I feel like I'm growing up here."

Opening Up Doors

It was the third year of our working together. We were concentrating on consolidating the positive changes that Celeste had already embarked upon. Her own studio was growing, as was her confidence. After recitals at her home for her young students, parents thanked her for making each of the kids feel "like a star." I encouraged her to begin joining music teachers' associations, explaining how that would open doors for both herself and her students, connecting her to the larger musical community and giving her students opportunities to perform and learn. Such advice, however, was in direct contradiction to that given by Madame Linsky, who didn't want Celeste to join groups outside Madame's own studio.

"She really wanted you all to herself," I said.

Celeste nodded in agreement. "Hers was a closed-off studio. I can see how this [joining organizations] would open doors and let air in." Then Celeste mentioned how raw she was feeling, craving time—alone time. "I don't want anyone near me these days."

"That makes perfect sense, Celeste," I replied, knowing, as anyone who has been in therapy knows, that the delicate, powerful process of awakening long-dormant aspects of the self requires a great deal of energy and care. Undergoing internal changes demands protection, as far as possible, from exposure to toxic or intrusive forces.

"And also," she sighed, "when I *think* of playing, I still get, you know"—her hands moved vertically in front of her—"well, I'm still not free!"

Looking at her hand gestures, I asked what was in front of her.

"A wall. . . ." She looked at the invisible wall in front of her, then broke out in a big smile. "It's a sheet of music. A sheet of music is holding me back from getting up and going to the piano!" she exclaimed with incredulity. I asked what she could do with that sheet.

"I can put it down." Once again, she marveled at the simplicity of the solution. But, thinking about it, she added: "Right before I said a sheet of music was preventing me from going to the piano, I wanted to say, 'a tablet.'"

The image of the daunting, awe-inspiring Ten Commandments appeared before me. I asked Celeste, "What does a tablet bring up for you?"

"The Ten Commandments."

"'Thou shalt not, thou shalt not, thou shalt not,'" I intoned in a deep, commanding voice. "Perhaps you will discover your own tablet at the piano that says, 'Thou shalt, thou shalt, thou shalt.'"

She went thoughtfully to the piano and played from a "thou shalt" stance, fullness and serenity in her face, grounded in her body. The tone was not forced, and she appeared to be "just playing" as if it was no big deal. Which made it a very big deal, indeed. When she finished, she remained quiet. She didn't ask for feedback. I didn't offer any.

She then asked if we could sight-read a Schubert four-hand piece. When counting got tricky, she froze, but it felt different from her absenting herself emotionally. I heard her say in a childlike, impetuous voice, "I can't do this. This is too hard." Immediately, I felt tiny stirrings of that urge to become a punishing figure. But then something extraordinary happened. I heard her say to herself, "That's okay. You can do this, Celeste. I know I can do this." She laughed nervously. She had pulled herself back to the present.

Enter the Dragon

Spring break came, and Celeste was away for two weeks. When she returned she sat at the keyboard, musing out loud. During the break she became cognizant of the importance of working on her issues, not only in therapy, but *through* her piano lessons. The demons that plagued her throughout her life were particularly conjured up in the sacred musical arena.

"When I play loudly I hear voices: They're telling me I can't do it." Though her judgmental voices took on an eerily disruptive, external aural presence, Celeste knew they were not real, recognizing that they were parts of herself, like the four-year-old. She also knew that it would behoove her to confront them.

"Tell me about those voices."

"Monsters. Ugly, big, scary . . ." She admitted being fearful she'd throw up when we talked about the demons.

"It feels like there's a dragon inside. A Chinese dragon like the one in the Chinese New Year parades."

I looked at her and, improbably, she appeared to become small, like Alice after eating the cookie. "Where are you? What's happening?"

"My mom's somewhere, maybe upstairs. I don't feel well . . . starting to feel queasy in my stomach."

"You're alone and lonely?"

"Yes. I want to be held. Sometimes when I felt panicky, my mother would maybe hold me. It makes me soooo angry . . ." Tears welled up.

"Celeste, don't dissipate your anger with tears now."

She stopped short and stared at me. "That anger, it feels like a dragon. It comes out of my mouth, gets bigger as it comes out."

"Can you let it out, even a little now?" And to my great surprise, Celeste let out a piercing scream, which, if it didn't frighten the dragon, certainly made me take a step back. Celeste, however, had a bemused expression on her face, cheeks flushed, eyes aglow. She stood there looking very impressed with herself and gave way to a big smile. I smiled back with raised eyebrows, wondering what Celeste was experiencing.

"Oh, my God! That felt incredible. I had no idea I could do that!" She continued standing as we discussed the demons-cum-dragon. Celeste, quite matter of factly, announced having made a discovery.

"Ever since we started talking about those demons, I've actually started feeling my body, I'm getting a real sense of what 'me' means. I've never felt connected to my body before." She looked angelic.

Smiling at her, I said: "I guess your hypochondria served the purpose of connecting you to your body any way it could." She got quiet, then calmly, slowly, turned to the keyboard, raised her arms and hands, gently lowered them onto a few notes. She let her hands remain on the notes while she listened to the dissipating resonance.

"This is extraordinary. We've done this so many times. . . . I'm finally feeling connected throughout my body, a sense of what it means to be Celeste, as a whole person, not individual parts. . . . I don't know what to say . . . this feels so profound."

The following week she reported having a dream where I told her to relax and she melted under the piano. But rather than panic, she felt calm when she awoke.

"I immediately knew how the dream fit into the larger picture of my life, that it was symbolic of my old fear of disappearing, of losing body parts. But I knew on waking that it would not actually happen. That it was a remnant of old stuff." She looked at the piano. "I'm also conscious about my crying. I thought about your telling me not to cry when I get angry. I got this picture of crying as a curling-up into myself, and not crying as being more engaged with the world. Well, I'm just musing out loud." Then she added, "I made a doctor's appointment and that's a *big* deal! I usually wait until I think I'm dying, but this time it's for a routine exam.

"I'm wondering what other ways there are to use what I'm learning here in the rest of my life," she pondered as she looked up from the piano and over it into the distance. But she was very present.

It was September, the beginning of our fourth year together.

"I hear differently. I'm seeing things I never noticed. It's a whole new world." Then, sadly: "How long it's taken."

"Mourning" had been an unnamed theme throughout our work: mourning for how long it had taken to connect to the world around her; for her derailed childhood with its lack of emotional nourishment; for the deprivation she felt at not having the requisite tools to become a musician. In addition, she had, no doubt, unconsciously internalized the keen sense of loss and mourning that other important adults in her life had experienced.

When I mentioned that, she replied with a big sigh. "Yes, of course, that must be true. My mom was such an unhappy person. It permeated the whole household. And oh, Madame. She lost her great love in the First World War—she never got over that. In fact, I know she kept his letters in a box tied with a beautiful yellow bow. I never want to be tied up like that," she plaintively, poetically said. And then, "I've got to do this work *at* the piano. Even if it's not about my becoming a pianist, there's too much that's tied to *here*," she said, pointing to the instrument.

I agreed. "You are discovering the healing power in the piano. Next time you feel like checking out of your body, touch the piano and focus on how that feels."

She quickly responded, conjecturing that there was anger and vengefulness underneath the "checking out."

"Anger at whom?" I pressed.

"My father . . . mother . . . Madame . . . *everyone* close to me."

"And me?"

She looked straight into my eyes and said, "No. Not anymore—I used to be, very. Finally I realized it had to do with other people." Then she immediately shut down. I could practically touch the wall that sprang into place. We both remarked on how quickly that happened.

"Anger scares me. Even just talking about it."

After having worked so hard, emotionally and musically, and having gotten used to making a big sound, Celeste entered a period of relative calm in which she addressed purely musical issues: the different touches at the keyboard, voicing, character and mood within pieces. She often accompanied herself with commentary, but it was less abusive than previously: "Well, that phrase needs work. . . . I need some hand-holding here . . . but not too much. . . ."

Chopin Nocturne: Security Blanket in C# Minor

Summer was approaching. Celeste's thirteen-year-old daughter would be going to summer camp, marking her first overnight departure from home, and both mother and daughter were nervous about the impending separation. In order not to let her anxiety spill over onto her daughter, Celeste grounded herself in her music.

"It's good modeling for your daughter, also, to see that Mom can take care of herself."

"Thanks. I really need to hear that. I don't want my anxiety to derail me, 'cause then I start getting angry and start blaming others for that anger and . . . well, it's the old stuff. I need to not do that anymore."

Celeste chose Chopin's *Nocturne in C# Minor, Op. 27* as her next piece, which soon became the symbol for her emerging sense of self. "This piece is for *me*, not you my teacher, not my mother, not for Madame. It's very important to me that I get it."

While studying the Nocturne for herself, Celeste reported constantly letting go of old pieces of behavior. Rather than seething when angry at her family, she soothed herself by taking a walk. Having been fearful both of being alone *and* of being away from home, this was not just new behavior, it was a double accomplishment. She also noted her diminishing need for control. If everything on her "to-do" list didn't get done, she no longer panicked.

With a broad smile, she added, "And when I have free time, I do *not* reach for the vacuum."

She turned to the Nocturne that was open on the music rack. Pointing to the sixth bar, which includes a big leap in the left hand, she said, in a slightly quaking voice, "I can't play this bar." I asked her to show me exactly where in the bar she had difficulty, and to play only those notes—in other words to de-glitchify. That meant paying attention, evaluating the exact location of the problem and not inflating the problem to seem too daunting to undertake.

Immediately, she realized that only a few notes, not the entire bar, were at issue. She plunged in. "Okay. Here goes. Starting with the third note in the left hand . . ." and she proceeded to spell out the notes and fingering. I noticed she played one note with a different finger than written on the music.

"I used a different fingering, didn't I?" She had noticed, a minor but important step. After I urged her to try both fingerings, we agreed her own was better for her hand than the editor's. She crossed out the editor's and penciled in her own.

Wanting to emphasize the import of what she was doing, I said, "You're beginning to trust yourself—not letting the editor of this edition dictate your fingering."

She sat quietly, slightly teary, and I guessed she was fighting the impulse to check out, as she often did after taking even a small, self-assertive stance. I saw her grounding herself by breathing calmly. Then she played a single note, held it and listened to the resonance as it died away. She was soothing herself and staying present.

Celeste surprised me by asking to hear my Rubinstein recording of the Chopin

Nocturne. Previously, she had always demurred at listening to recordings of great artists for fear of being discouraged. But after we listened, she quietly said, "I can do this," then turned back to the Nocturne, grounded herself and began to play. Undeterred by wrong notes, she engaged in her usual commentary. "That wasn't right . . . I'm not going to stop . . . That didn't sound bad. . . ." And then, "I feel empowered by my anger."

When she finished she said, "This piece is my . . ." As she searched for the right word, the word that came to my mind was "gateway." But Celeste hit on her own truth: "security blanket."

"I had a dream last night," she announced at the next lesson. "I was holding a baby and trying to make my way through a room strewn with overturned furniture, like desks and chairs." She made zigzag motions with her hand. "There were so many barriers. I just held the baby close to my chest as I tried to make my way through."

Celeste presented the dream and then quickly turned back to playing the piano, leaving me to remark to myself how her vision mirrored what was transpiring within her: how her protective embracing of the baby paralleled the care she was finally bestowing on her own, newly emerging and still-vulnerable self. And how the emotional roadblocks that angered her were transformed into furniture she could sidestep as she moved forward in her work. Talk about the mind–body connection!

As she turned back to the Nocturne, I asked, "Why don't you play the Nocturne as a lullaby for the baby?"

As the Nocturne took on more of its nocturnal character, Celeste appeared to be enjoying the unselfconsciousness that denotes absorption in the music. But that very freedom frightened her. As she got to the few bars where only one hand plays, her feeling of exposure overwhelmed her. She looked at the clock.

"It's time. I have to go." And she flew out the door.

When she returned the following week, she walked directly to the piano and opened the Nocturne.

Since the Nocturne was such a catalytic force behind the work Celeste did, this might be a good time to say a few words about it.

The structure of the Chopin Nocturne, or night-piece, has three sections—ABA. Section A is tranquil and opens with a beautiful melody in the right hand accompanied by a flowing, lefthand pattern. There is a short transitional bridge to a contrasting middle section, B, of more intensity and drama. In B, the right-hand aria is transformed from a singing line to a succession of rhythmically incessant chords played increasingly faster and louder. The turbulent left hand propels the motion in a contrasting rhythm. The middle section then segues into the last, a nostalgic revisiting of A. All parts, including the transitions, possess their own character. Bridges have their own challenge, as well: not as important musically as the sections they connect, they are nevertheless an integral part of the music, to be incorporated seamlessly and musically.

Although there are challenges embedded in the outside, aria-like sections (A), the middle section (B) is flagrant about its challenges. No wonder Celeste would come to a screeching halt at the prospect of playing it with drive and intensity! She jumped away from the piano with bristling energy when she came to that section. I asked her if she wanted to move to it while I played it. She nodded yes. As I played, I heard her accompany her movement with commentary.

"Anger. Lots of anger . . . everyone putting me in a cage, defining who I am. . . ."

I asked her to keep moving, as if from the cage she'd been put in. I played the whole Nocturne, purposely not looking at her so she wouldn't feel intimidated.

"Stay in the cage, explore it . . . discover if there's a safe way to leave it."

It surprised me that she let me play the entire Nocturne. When she stopped moving, she reported on her private dance. "I was little . . . and there was a lot of stuff in that cage. Furniture, fabric, knickknacks. . . . I don't want any of it. I want to get rid of it."

"What's the safest way for you to get rid of it?"

She looked pensive. "I'll create a glass house where the inside and outside easily drift into each other. . . . I can see the big trees from inside and go out to touch them. When I'm cold I'll walk outside into the sun."

Without entirely grasping the logic of her response, I declared, "That way you create safety for yourself, both inside and out."

Once again, I played as she moved. "This is so totally different," she whispered.

Then she entered the rhythmically driven middle section. The air in the room changed; anger descended like a deus ex machina on stage. In newly emphatic tones she said, "I want to tear everything up, tear the fabric, destroy the furniture—I want to throw it all away. It's like a knife in my stomach, the carpet pulled out from under me. I'm scared. . . ." She hesitated.

". . . of . . ." I prompted.

". . . that my body parts will scatter."

I stopped playing and turned toward her with a determined look. This moment held so much energy it needed to be harnessed. Emphatically I said, "I want you to find a way right now to make sure your body remains completely intact." I paused a short moment. "Can you stay inside your body while I play a few bars from that [middle, dramatic] section?" Our eyes locked. Hesitantly, she nodded yes. I watched her carefully as she moved to my playing. Despite her frightened look, I sensed that she stayed in her body while listening to what had been anger-provoking music. She was exhausted at the end.

I, however, was energized at having witnessed the visceral relationship between anger and rhythm. Holding herself back from playing rhythmically was the counterpart for Celeste to holding feelings in check so as not to be overwhelmed by them. But without finding her own rhythm, her own feelings, she could not move forward. My excitement grew the more I thought about it; and I wondered how that session in which anger had played such a palpable role would play out during the week for Celeste.

The next week she walked in and, as usual, greeted me graciously. I returned the greeting and looked at her expectantly. She didn't say anything. When I mentioned being curious about what she thought of the anger she had brought up the week before, she awkwardly smiled but managed to grimace at the same time. I realized she'd forgotten about it.

"Oh, dear. Thank you for bringing it up. I need to keep hearing that because I can't hold onto my anger, it seems. Last week I completely forgot I was angry by the time I got home. Then in therapy it came up, and then once again—it disappeared." Quickly turning back to the piano, Celeste said, "Right now I want to play that section in the Nocturne and have you just witness." I moved slightly back to give her space, knowing that using the piano was often Celeste's preferred mode of communication when verbal expression proved inadequate.

She dove into the Nocturne's rhythmically driven middle section with a big, aggressive sound. To my happy surprise she went through almost to the end. Then she stopped. She was shaking and said she felt nauseated.

Gently but firmly I said, "Celeste, I want you to keep playing, and keep your body together."

Taking up the gauntlet, she threw herself back into the piece. I heard her say from time to time, "I am together." Her overall demeanor was determined and calm. And then suddenly I noticed something I'd never witnessed before: Her eyes were off the page and on the keyboard—she was actually playing from memory. For the first time, she played straight through the middle section and into the transition leading to the last section with no mistakes. When she stopped, she said she had not been thinking at all while she played. "I didn't even wonder what *you* were thinking."

I asked her to play the piece again right away. I didn't want this to be a single, isolated moment that, while it felt good, could then be forgotten—like her anger.

She did so with aplomb, speaking through her playing as was her custom, sounding confident and fluid. Then I noticed something else: I was listening to her with my eyes closed. I often listen that way with students; it allows me to concentrate more on the music. But with Celeste I usually remained observant, alert to any nuance in manner that might herald emotional disruption. Now for the first time, I was sitting back and listening with enjoyment.

She was visibly exhausted when she ended. I asked how she would like to spend the remaining minutes of her lesson. I should have anticipated her response.

"That's enough. I'm going home and taking a nap."

Celeste and I spent another year and a half together. She was increasingly able to observe herself and soothe herself on the spot when anxious. She no longer felt timid telling people she taught beginners lest they assume she wasn't good enough to teach advanced students. When asked, she replied, "I'm a piano teacher. I specialize in teaching beginners."

Self-assurance was mirrored in dreams. "I had a dream last night. I was with strangers who were professional pianists. We were testing a piano to see if it was good. Everyone played in turn, and they said it was fabulous. After I took my turn

I said, 'You're *all* wrong.'" Her raised eyebrows and ear-to-ear smile revealed her sense of triumph: Not only had she not panicked at the prospect of playing before other musicians, but she had held her own against the "experts."

Most happily for our work, her self-assurance was mirrored in lessons, which were becoming less entangled with emotional derailment and more about making music. Celeste was able to sustain making big, powerful sounds without retreating. Comments I'd make were heard as comments, not judgments.

When she rushed through quarter-note chords in a Chopin Prelude, she observed: "Yes. I'm still afraid to hear myself—I cut myself off when I shorten the chords." She didn't shut down when I told her to "live inside the space of those quarter notes" and to "keep rhythmically steady by breathing *in* on the 'and' [the silent part] of the chord, and breathing *out* as you play the next chord." I accompanied her by noisily inhaling and exhaling alongside her.

Initially intimidated when I discussed how notes in a phrase were related to each other and how to shape them, she explained, flushed with animation: "In the past when I played, notes would stick out. I wouldn't understand why it sounded wrong. This is exciting." And the epiphany, after an afternoon of listening and playing: "I felt it! I felt the connection to the music. I experienced *hearing* myself play, I experienced *feeling* the music. . . ." She looked off in wonderment. "I don't want to play with mistakes anymore. I want to be an adult at the keyboard," she said with a sheepish grin.

I decided to demonstrate how I practice de-glitchifying (minus the cursing I often do when practicing alone). I showed Celeste an actual problem I had in a piece I was learning, and proceeded to practice in front of her. All the while, I spoke out loud, describing the process. First, I figured out what I needed to do. (Refinger the five-note passage whose previous fingering prevented proper phrasing.) Then I calmed myself, and slowly played it correctly with easy hands, giving myself helpful verbal prompts ("thumb goes on B") to reinforce sensory input (looking at how hands looked on keyboard when playing correctly; feeling internally how it felt when the phrase was smooth). Assured of the solution, I practiced it correctly many times. Then I practiced putting it back into the piece. Many times. Then I got up and moved so as not to get stiff.

"That really hit home," Celeste said soberly, half-smiling, "paying attention, taking time." After a minute she added, "I'm feeling so much energy, exhilaration even, feeling all of myself present. It's like pulling the dragon out. . . . It's so different from cleaning house."

The Music Continues

It had been a while since Celeste and I were able to engage in banter, teacher to teacher, and woman to woman, rather than as judge and student. Celeste allowed herself to air her curiosity about me and asked what I was doing besides teaching. I told her I was writing another book—"my second and last," I said with a laugh, referring to this book. I did not elaborate and consciously avoided mentioning the title I had in mind for it. There was warmth in the interchange, reflecting the shifts that had taken place.

She returned the following week and related this dream. "I dreamed there was a couch alongside the piano, but you were sitting there," pointing to me sitting next to the piano in my teacher's chair. "And we were just talking about music and playing the piano."

Her words took me by surprise. It felt as if Celeste's dream had somehow validated my work, work that had often played tricks on me, and in which I felt I often stumbled. It humbled me to hear them, and at the same time I was so grateful.

Then one day Celeste quietly walked in, greeted me with her gracious smile and asked if we could sit in the chairs away from the piano. She told me she was going to take a break from lessons. She quietly revealed that she had seen Madame on one of her recent trips home. Celeste had been nervous when she called Madame, but felt impelled to tell her about her musical development. I suspected she was hoping for Madame's blessing on her forging ahead. Instead, Madame had said, "I knew you would leave me someday." Celeste bent down to kiss her when she left; Madame stayed seated, eyes looking forward. Celeste showed no obvious emotion while she related the encounter, but I felt heartsick as I imagined the scene.

Celeste continued: "I realized it was a very important moment in my life. First of all, I didn't 'check out' as I left, which I noticed and was pleased about. Then, my reaction was, 'I don't know how I feel. Margret will help me find out.' Then I said, 'I need to sit with this and find out what I'm feeling, myself.' And I discovered that, yes, of course, at first it was dejection and sadness and loss. But it also had a tiny spark of renewal, of freedom. It was a pivotal moment in which I realized I was going forward. I could walk out, with or without her blessing, and feel sad and still be okay. And I had to sit with that myself sometimes at the piano, and often while walking—and just let it be."

With an ease that had been long in coming, Celeste continued:

"You know, I went from the frying pan into the fire when I first came here. I've taken lessons continually without a break since I started when I was young. I continued without interruption with Madame and I brought all my baggage here and continued as I'd always done, with my mask on, fooling myself, unconscious."

As I watched her, my mind was racing. First thought: Have I failed her? Then: Was she ready to quit? Would she hold on to what we'd accomplished together? And, then, what will I say to show my support and confidence in her?

"I was not afraid to come and tell you," she stated, and I heard pride in her voice. She was calm and looked softly radiant. I realized that that was a tribute to us both. She had taken an adult-like stance in asserting what was best for herself. And in so doing she understood that my own strength was not entwined with hers, that she needn't continue seeing me in order for me to remain whole. We embraced our good-byes, two women who had worked hard and grown, and knew there would be more challenges ahead.

Since then, whenever I think of Celeste, I hear *Clair de Lune*. It is the piece that quietly continues after it ends.

Postscript

Celeste responded after I sent her this chapter to read:

> *It was such a gift, the opportunity to do what I did, working with you. As I read about the Nocturne work, I realize I'd wanted to forget all about it. I love teaching beginners: I made a schedule that works for me—teaching everyday between 2 and 8, except weekends. I take 45 minutes before I start each day— it's my sacred time, all to myself. I'm always thinking of new ways to be creative with the kids, and the other night I crept into the dark living room, sat at the piano and improvised. It was the first time: it felt wonderful.*

[FOUR]

ALEXANDER - A TRINITY OF SELVES

I should be utterly lost if I knew where I was going.[26]
— Georges Braque, twentieth-century French painter

The man on the phone was carefully explaining why he'd called me.

"I read the review of your book in the *California Music Journal*. I've always admired the reviewer, Ms.___, so I thought I should find out more about your work. I'm reading your book now, and it's really making sense." As he went on at length, I was smiling to myself at the unique way the unconscious has of guiding us. For in fact, the review had not been written by the reviewer the caller named, but by another. If the caller had noticed that, would his response have been the same?

Alexander was a handsome man, nearly six feet tall, in his late thirties and impeccably dressed. I noticed his hands immediately—beautiful, supple, my ideal of the pianist's hands. They reminded me of my father's hands, which had often been remarked on, and the first subject of my picture taking when I was five. My father had wanted to become a pianist when he studied in Warsaw before the Second World War, but stopped playing altogether when his teacher told him he would never play like Horowitz. Thus, I had always had a close-up view of the artist manqué, the artist unfulfilled, and momentarily projected onto Alexander the potential for greatness that escaped my father. Looking back, I wonder if that projection influenced my initial work with him. Over the four years we were to work together, I would need to reconsider my view of him on several occasions in order to better align myself with his experience.

Alexander began speaking as soon as he entered our first meeting, and continued speaking without pause for that entire session and many subsequent sessions. He sat erect. No matter the content of what he said, his tone was matter-of-fact, his facial expression unchanged. Alexander spent those first sessions relating how he had taught himself as a child to play the piano by watching and listening to others, of his acceptance at twelve years of age into the preparatory division of the conservatory near his home, and of his subsequent graduation from college with a major in music.

He talked about his large teaching studio in a city about an hour's drive from my own, of the youngsters he taught and the difficulties he had with their oppositional parents. He talked about his challenges in performing and his longing for a sense of ease in playing. Alexander launched into a detailed description of all the books he had read about piano playing, minutely analyzing various technical methods. He spoke about his frustration at never producing the sound he heard within himself, and the need to continually disrupt his practicing to perseverate over perfecting a few notes.

As I pieced together the multiple fragments of information imparted during those initial sessions, I sought a tentative framework with which to approach Alexander's presenting issues. At some point I thought I had grasped the basic dilemma: With his natural talent and keen musical ear, the young, self-taught Alexander had become sufficiently proficient at the keyboard to gain entry into a prestigious music school. Once admitted, the gaps in his musical foundation may have been obscured. Undoubtedly, I surmised, Alexander had missed some essential steps in the learning process, steps—such as basic sight-reading, hand position, practice techniques—that most children taking lessons at an early age are guided through. Though he was unconscious of these gaps, they confronted him at the keyboard, and Alexander would try to compensate for them intellectually by reading and analyzing.

The solution seemed simple: I would help him fill in those missing technical and musical gaps by giving him the necessary tools to achieve what he had sought through reading about them. I knew (or presumed to know) that if he agreed to this work, if he practiced what I taught him, he would become the pianist he craved to be, the pianist I had projected onto him. It should not be a long process.

There was merit in my diagnosis, but I was wrong about the appropriate path to pursue. Regardless of the straightforward solution I imagined, Alexander loquaciously steered me toward his own agenda. Though it was incumbent on me to follow Alexander's path, I occasionally slipped into trying to control our direction. When I made practical suggestions, he politely balked and steered me back to discussions of what wasn't working. I became better at catching my own impatience at not moving quickly enough to our—that is, *my*—destination. Sitting across from Alexander, I often needed to take a page regarding optimum performance from my own book: Sit quietly, breathe slowly and focus on him by listening, watching and noticing my internal responses.

Listening to the Wall

Letting go of my agenda allowed our sessions to flow more easily, and serendipitously enabled Alexander to pursue a line of discovery that led to a pleasant surprise.

I had come to infer that Alexander, despite coming to talk to me, had scant expectation of finding release from his habitual constraints. He referred to these constraints as a "plague." At our fourth session we had the following exchange.

"I'm not sure why I can't play the way I want, not get past a certain point. It's like there's this—well, I know this is going to sound silly, but a wall in front of me, and I can't get rid of that feeling of being walled in. I would really like to get rid of it. When I play I . . ."

"Wait," I interjected, knowing he could continue talking for a long time. "Let's stay with that wall. Can you describe it?"

He laughed, looking perplexed by the question.

I prompted, "Where is the wall exactly? Is it smooth, high?"

"Well, let's see . . . " he said, capitulating to this unfamiliar method of questioning. "It's metallic, about this far in front of me," his hands measuring about two feet.

"Tell me more. When did it first come into your life?"

More serious now, he searched for the answer. "When I was about seven."

"What happened in your life when you were seven?"

Alexander told me that when he was seven he and his parents moved to a small town. It was not the ideal environment for a boy who realized he was different from other boys, more sensitive and prone to crying.

"So the wall protected you then?"

He looked perplexed. "I guess."

"Without it, what might have happened?"

His hands went out, palms up in a gesture that seemed to say the answer was obvious. "Well, I would've been beaten up by the bully next door . . . the kids would have constantly insulted me." His hands fell, while his eyes looked up. A minute went by. "So, the wall was a barrier between me and being hurt by the rest of the kids. Hmmm."

The following week, Alexander couldn't wait to tell me his surprise: The wall had spoken to him at home. "As I sat down at the piano, I heard it say, 'I'm really a part of you, I'm here to help.'"

Wanting to celebrate the moment, he plunged into playing the Chopin *Berceuse* for me. Barely had the last note died away than he began the litany of all that had gone wrong. "I should be able to play this on any piano at any time. That's what performers must do."

I raised my eyebrows. "Yes, performers with years of practicing hours a day, who give concerts all over on different pianos. You have unrealistic expectations for yourself." I took a moment. "I wonder how holding onto unrealistic expectations serves you?"

"They don't. They make me miserable."

"I'm not so sure. Could you ask the wall?"

As soon as I said that, Alexander's face lit up and his eyes widened. I watched in anticipation; I'd not seen this expression on his face before.

"Something incredible just happened. . . . I got an immediate response. My wall said that unrealistic expectations help me by keeping me from going out—from exposing myself to ridicule, as a sensitive man, as a pianist . . . as a gay man."

We looked at each other. It was the first time he'd said "gay."

But what had most impressed Alexander at that moment was the immediacy of the internal response he'd gotten from the wall.

"The wall answered me immediately. It didn't make me work hard to get a response. This is really turning me around. I've always had to labor, always thought the only way to get anything was by working hard. I mean, my parents were immigrants, they came with nothing, didn't speak the language. They slaved to keep the family going. I learned that life was not supposed to be easy. But the wall just answered me without making me work hard."

I saw him go inside himself, seeming to digest the experience.

As he left my studio he looked at my dog lying under the piano and asked, "Does the dog ever get let out?"

"Yes," I responded, and added silently, "and so will you."

Hidden Selves: The Fear of Being Seen

Alexander was anxious for me to understand him, to really see who he was. He described the image he had of himself as being composed of three separate selves: his musician self, his gay self and the self he presented to the rest of the mostly heterosexual world. Each self was walled off from interacting with the others, precluded from entering the others' domain. He was aware of these separate selves; they were not dissociated parts of himself.

Alexander packed our sessions with as many details of his story as he could. He related how his parents had escaped the Iron Curtain when Alexander was four and his sister Ilona was seven. Like other immigrants, his parents worked long hours, had little time to learn English and relied on their children as intermediaries in the new country. His father took pride in being self-sufficient, and never asked anyone outside his nuclear family for help. Though his parents didn't understand Alexander's temperament or love of music, they at least did not prevent him from teaching himself to play the piano that a kindly, elderly neighbor gave him, nor did they thwart his auditioning at twelve for the nearby conservatory.

Alexander, blessed with natural ability, spent untold hours teaching himself the few pieces he played at the audition. Once accepted, he was motivated to work even harder, presenting himself admirably at his lessons. Thus, no one realized how little he actually knew about the fundamental technique of playing the piano.

It may sound strange to the reader that a competent classical pianist can reach a high level of achievement without basic training, but it is not a rare occurrence.

Such musicians are remarkably talented, have a wonderful ear and possess an insatiable drive to play. Music becomes entwined with psychic survival. If there is early access to an instrument, they might begin by picking out music by ear. With exquisite sensitivity to sound, they ceaselessly work at the instrument to approximate what they have heard. If the opportunity arises to attend performances, they watch performers for clues as to how hands and arms behave while performing, without necessarily understanding the relation of those movements to the performer's interpretation of the music. Often there is a gap in learning to read music, as that can be harder to achieve on one's own than imitating sound. But, native talent facilitates sounding "musical" to the outside world.

The emphasis on listening and producing sound can be a blessing and a curse in these instances. It is a blessing because sound is, of course, the essential ingredient in producing music. For people like Alexander, schooled early in imitating sound rather than in reading music, sound is the grounding element. As he emphatically told me, "The notes on the page are foreign objects, like aliens. I pay attention only to the sound."

While sound can be grounding, it can also be distracting if it becomes, as it did for Alexander, the single focus in playing. Alexander habitually aborted his playing because he was dissatisfied with his sound. And, alert to a family ethic that stressed self-reliance and independence, he turned to educating himself to correct what was missing in his playing. In reading about, experimenting with and studying different pianists' approaches—all worthy educational pursuits—Alexander sought to fill the gaps on his own that he instinctively recognized.

Alexander spoke with energy about his lessons at college with Ms. K., a teacher well known for being demanding and precise. "She was a wonderful teacher, but she never knew what it cost me to learn those Beethoven Sonatas and Chopin Etudes. She intimidated me, so I went home and practiced until I couldn't practice anymore. Then she'd say, 'When I was your age I could learn that in three weeks.' That made me think that if I were any good I should also be able to learn and memorize a piece immediately. But she didn't show us how." Alexander's glance shifted briefly from looking at me to looking down and in that moment I caught a look of sadness and loss, but none of the anger that I myself was experiencing while listening to him.

"Did your teacher ever tell you at what age she began lessons and how many hours a day she'd been practicing all her life?" I asked.

"She told her students that she'd been playing since she was three when her mother began teaching her in Vienna. She practiced hours every day for years."

Before I could address the difference between his mentor's years of hard work and his belief that he should be able to play effortlessly, he went on. "I'm remembering how easy it was for me to get an answer from the wall a few weeks ago, when it told me it was there to protect me."

Following his train of thought, I asked: "What do you think you did then that allowed you to get an easy answer?"

"I guess recognizing a part of myself that was hidden before."

I leaned in toward him. "Do you imagine there's another part of you still hidden that needs recognizing?"

He thought quietly for a few moments. "I don't know." His eyes looked away. But, glimpsing their rapid movement, I sensed we were on fertile soil. "What were you just thinking?" I asked.

"Well, this is off the topic, but I was just remembering a bumper sticker I recently saw: 'Proud parent of a student of the month. . . .' I was once student of the month. It felt wonderful. It was one of the few times I felt deserving, worthy."

I was trying to keep pace with the sequence of his associations. "Are you saying the part of you that's hidden is the 'worthy student part'?" There was quiet. As he looked at me intently, I continued. "That's interesting because the student's responsibility is to learn and benefit from other people's knowledge. It's not necessarily to bear the burden of discovering everything for himself." I let a moment of silence go by. "Maybe that student part of you wants out again so you don't have to work so hard at reinventing the wheel at the piano." I sat back. I was talking too much. He looked distracted and I thought, "He isn't having any of this."

An Assault on My Essence

Several weeks later, Alexander entered my studio, scowling. Without his usual greeting, and without pausing for breath between sentences, he related this story.

"I don't know why I'm so angry today, but I know I have to tell you about it. The parent of one of my students hasn't paid on time. I feel so devalued by this

83

person, so disrespected. Just like the parent who thought her child was entitled to a makeup lesson when she wasn't. I have a strict studio policy about payments and makeups. I told her I couldn't reschedule and explained it was because I had to do other important things in the hours I wasn't teaching." Several issues were wrapped up in his words, but I chose to address the last item he mentioned.

"You know, Alexander, you don't really need to justify yourself. It doesn't matter whether you do important things or not with your time. That's your business. Perhaps you could graciously but firmly refer her to your policy and say you're sorry, but that's the policy?"

He looked up as if he'd been hit. "Just hearing that statement—no need to justify myself—gave me a big jolt. I feel I *always* have to justify myself . . . like all the times my family invited me to family gatherings and asked all kinds of questions about my life—if I was dating, when I'd get married, have children. Even though I come with Gino, my partner, they treat him as my friend and don't recognize us as a couple. It's an assault on my very essence. Answering questions was torture, so I stopped going to those parties." There was a hint of real anger as he spoke.

"It sounds like your family doesn't want to acknowledge that you're gay."

"But that's who I am!" His voice rose several pitches. "They aren't seeing *me*. It feels like I was never seen—as a boy or as a man." Then his voice fell. "I feel so vulnerable." Alexander had put a halt to his growing exasperation, scared perhaps by the intensity of the underlying anger.

"So now when someone questions you about something you stand for, like your teaching policy, it feels like an assault against your very being, like once again you are not being seen," I confirmed.

"Yes. That's exactly right. Why can't they just accept me? Why do I have to explain myself, or my policy?" Alexander's voice echoed with the complex timbre of a child's whine mingled with an adult's anger.

I assured him that his feelings made complete sense. But, I reminded him, "These parents are approaching you in your professional capacity. They are not approaching your 'essence' or you as a gay man. You are first and foremost their child's piano teacher, so it's important to respond to them from that place. Even when they're unreasonable." I paused for breath. "Can you . . ."

He interrupted. "But it feels so hopeless, this constant experiencing of assaults.

Like the plague, I feel like it's never going to change." He had used the word *plague* before to encapsulate feelings of inevitability, helplessness and shame when old wounds got triggered. I hoped an intervention based on exercises he'd read about and we'd discussed might empower him when faced with such deeply rooted sensations.

"I'm wondering," I continued, "if you could find a way to respond that honors yourself as the teacher, as well as your students' parents."

I could see that my words hit a vital spot. As he looked at me intently, I suggested, "First, let's go over the breathing exercise from my book."

"The Calming Light exercise. I know it. Okay."

"Good. I suggest you practice it throughout the day, wherever you are, until you can immediately cue yourself to calm yourself." He nodded assent. "Now, think of a statement that honors both you and the parents." He took a long moment, then nodded "yes." I didn't ask what it was. But before I could continue, he blurted out, "But what if they argue with me?"

Remembering the powerful word "nevertheless" I'd read about in a child-rearing book, I responded: "Stay connected with yourself by breathing to your cue and say something like, 'I understand what you're saying. *Nevertheless,* my policy is clear on missed lessons. I'd be happy to go over it with you again.' If the parent argues, you keep your gracious smile, stay grounded and repeat, '*Nevertheless,* my policy, etc. . . .' Then," I added slyly, "you can come here and scream all you want." We exchanged smiles. Then we rehearsed a scene with me as a parent demanding a makeup lesson for my child who had missed a lesson. He took a few seconds for a calming breath, looked at me and answered.

"I've worked hard to make a fair office policy. I'd be glad to review it with you, but I don't make up lessons except for illness." He was a bit awkward, but this was his first stab at responding as a professional, not as a man whose essence had been assaulted. He would hone the skill with practice.

Three months into our work, Alexander reported a dream he had the night before our session. "I was in an old wooden boat, crossing a body of water. When we landed I was afraid." A moment. "I think it's about our work here." I raised my eyebrows in question. "It makes me anxious sometimes, realizing I don't know what's ahead. I know what we're doing here is right because I'm feeling different. But I can't clearly see the future. Like getting off the boat in a different country."

Another moment. He smiled as he looked at me. "But I'm having a better time with my students—I'm not so controlling and rigid. I'm also not so defensive with their parents when they ask me questions."

Complex and Distressing Issues of the Soul

That summer, Alexander attended a piano conference, and while there he had a profound set of experiences he was eager to relate.

While half listening during a master class, he found himself doodling in his notebook. Looking closely, he sensed the doodles were about his work with me and the long process of discovering the "complex and distressing issues of the soul," as he eloquently had written, and of how his trust was slowly developing in the work and in me. He was seeing how his demons, the parts of himself he felt were holding him back, actually served as guardians against his opening up. During the conference he had a dream.

"I'm playing the piano and suddenly I get up and leave, but a part of me remains at the keyboard, playing. That part is a woman, and she plays the whole *Berceuse* through without stopping, without being disturbed by any inner voices of judges or critics. My piano dreams have always been distressing, but this one wasn't. It was marvelous."

I asked him to dramatize each of his dream roles, playing the piano as himself and as the woman.

He felt a visceral link to the latter. "She plays beautifully, easily. Just enjoying the music. She says, 'Just let me be.'"

I prodded him to ask her to elaborate.

"She says she resides in my heart."

"And where does she come from?"

"All my piano teachers. My three women teachers." Those were the primary women in his life who had facilitated his passion for music; thus, this dream heralded a big step in Alexander's full acceptance of his own feminine/sensitive/musical/gay self.

The following week, Alexander came in with a long piece, half of which he had memorized. "I know this wasn't my homework but I wanted to play this for you."

"And your immediate goal?" I queried.

"I just want to see if I can get through it without feeling inadequate or undeserving," he responded. I knew my goal was to listen.

After he played, I said nothing. The music had been full of mistakes of notes and timing. The image that emerged as I listened was of someone climbing Mount Everest in thin clothing and sandals, unprepared for such a task.

Looking solemn, Alexander said: "I think that what was behind my playing just now was to show my very worst side, my horrible playing side, just to get through it."

"And still be accepted by me?" I asked softly.

He nodded, yes.

My own thoughts wandered to Alexander's relationship with his mother. In retrospect I can see how showing his "worst side" to me, an older woman—like his mother—was a plea to his mother for acceptance, no matter how he played, no matter who he was. But, rather than comment on his transference, I asked too abruptly: "How would your relation with your mother change, if you were to play the way you wanted?"

Quickly, anger tinged with sadness: "It wouldn't . . . unfortunately. She wouldn't get the importance of it for me. I'd feel very lonely." The expression on his face became that of a young boy. His gaze strayed and seemed to fix on the tree outside the window. I could palpably sense his loneliness, as well as his fear that being angry was an act of disloyalty against a parent who had struggled so hard in life.

"Is it possible your *not playing* to your satisfaction keeps alive the hope—the hope of a young boy—that one day you *will* play perfectly like a good boy, and then she *will* 'get it,' get you? Does *not* playing well serve to stave off loneliness?" Forlornly, he looked out the window. After a few moments the associations he had been making in his mind about women, family, loneliness were divulged.

"My grandmother—my father's mother—is sick, probably dying."

"Are you close to your grandmother?"

"Well, I love her because she is my grandmother. But she was a cruel lady. Catholic in the worst sense of the word. I remember hearing how she made my father sit outside completely nude when he was young so everyone passing by could see him because he had said a dirty word.

"Then there's my mother's side." He sat forward, an enigmatic expression on his face. As I listened, I wondered how many different feelings were battling internally as he divulged the shameful side of his history. "*Her* mother got pregnant at seventeen, but when my mother also got pregnant at seventeen, her mother kicked her out of the house. She had to live with my father on his mother's farm—the same farm where he had been shamed as a child. My father had a reputation for being wild, drinking. His mother told *my* mother to get an abortion when she got pregnant again. I guess she was worried they'd never leave her place if they remained poor and kept having kids.

"My older sister, who I really love, got pregnant before she was married and had an abortion. When I came out to her about twenty years ago, I was hoping I'd be able to do so with everyone in the family. But after I told my mother, she told me to stop talking about it. Good Catholic family, so many secrets." He continued without pause.

"I want to talk about this stuff with them, and I keep thinking about what you said some time ago—to talk in a way that honors me and them. I want them to understand me, but also I'm grappling with understanding their hurt, like when I don't come to family gatherings, or keep to myself." A moment's pause, a glance at the sun coming through the blinds. "But I really don't want to be talking about this here anymore. Here, this should only be for my music."

"I don't see these issues as separate. As long as there's a need to talk about them, they are part of your music, as well."

He looked surprised. Then sighed. "That's a kindness I never experienced. Just being accepted for my entire being. Maybe that's why I need to do that work here."

The following week he reported dreaming that he had played his family's favorite song from the old country, and they were singing along. He looked almost beatific relating the dream, but then he teared up and said the strangest thing. "I've always thought of you—I hope this doesn't make you mad—as the devil. As the devil who resides between each of my fingers."

"Meaning the harsh critic, the severe judge ruling against you?"

"Yes, exactly. It's still so hard to let myself believe in, to let you be kind to me, not judgmental." His body appreciably softened from his normally tightly held stance. "To let myself be really seen. Normally I feel like I'm in a dark room."

"What was the room like?" I wondered aloud.

"It's crowded with junk and dust. It's very oppressive. I can't see—it's very dark."

Wanting him to continue his train of thought, I asked, "How did you get in that room?"

His eyes looked down. He was used to such questions by now. "I walked in."

"From where?"

"Another room."

"Was there any light there?"

"Yes." Brows knit, he continued concentrating on his internal scene.

"If you leave the door open, does the light from that other room let you see into the dark room?"

A moment, then: "Yes. The light helps. I can start identifying the stuff in the room. Junk, tons of old papers and furniture. . . . I can see a way out."

The following week, he reported this dream: "I was driving with friends over a hill I really love. I see these houses that I like a lot, and I'm especially drawn to one in particular—not too big or unusual—kind of like your house. And I wanted to stop but my friends didn't want to.

"So later on I come back myself, and go to the door of this house and it's open a crack and as I get closer the door widens. It's pretty dark, but I'm not afraid. I know there's a room with a light on somewhere in the house and I just go toward it."

When he stopped, he glanced out the large window next to us, where light radiated into the room. Alexander seemed absorbed in thought, which precluded interruption. So I mused on the beautiful description in the dream of his internal progress: from feeling enclosed in a dark, oppressive room, or by a wall, to being in a house that holds the promise of light. Suddenly a broad smile overtook his face as he haltingly spoke.

"I wonder . . . is this the house . . . that I walk through to my future?" An expression of wonderment on his face. Then, as he followed his train of thought, he spoke of his feelings for Helga, one of the three important women in his musical life. Helga had been a friend until her death at eighty, two years before I met Alexander. She had loved music passionately and lived life fully. And she had loved Alexander unconditionally.

"I think of Helga—her grand pianos that she made such sacrifices to own. Her garden. Her house. If I love a place," he said, inadvertently casting his eyes around him, "I memorize every detail. It feels so sad not to have Helga's house there anymore."

"Would you like to play something for Helga, from the feelings you hold for her?"

Without a word, he turned back to the piano and played one of Helga's favorite pieces, a Chopin *Nocturne*. His playing mirrored the sadness and nostalgia he had expressed. I was moved by the genuine passion in his playing. It seemed to have opened the door further onto his internal lighted room, and in the following week he spoke of being happy for the first time in a very long time.

Gay Self, Piano-Teacher Self

Alexander had spoken of himself as living in three separate selves: his gay self, his musician self and the self he presented to the heterosexual world. He said he felt whole at our sessions, but otherwise played one role at a time and hid the others. Slowly, though, Alexander's gay self was coming out of hiding. As our session was ending one day, he blurted out how surprised he was by his response to a young male student who, while innocently talking about all kinds of love, asked if a boy could marry a boy.

"'I don't know,' I told him. 'That's probably not likely.' That was such a risk. Before I would have told him, 'Absolutely not.'"

I asked if there were anything else he would have liked to have said.

"Next time I'll say, 'I don't see why not.'" He looked saddened. "I wish it were easier just to be myself." As he got up to leave, he turned to me and said, "I have to switch now, get rid of my sad face so I can teach with my happy teacher's face."

That bothered me and I quickly responded. "Alexander, you don't need to cut yourself off from feelings. Can you imagine allowing yourself to feel your sadness, and let it quietly enrich your lessons, without, of course, imposing it on your students?" His eyes opened wide. I knew from the startled look on his face that he would mull this over at his leisure. He had long lived by automatically cutting himself off from feelings deemed "inappropriate," dictated by his rigid sense of socially imposed boundaries. The role of piano teacher did not include revealing feelings during lessons.

Still, fluidity was evolving in Alexander's compartmentalized worlds as he loosened the armor of each of his selves, occasionally bantering with his piano students and answering their questions with ease and humor. Parents' questions about their children's lessons no longer elicited feelings of having his essence attacked.

In addition, his social horizons were broadening as his view of the gay life was undergoing change, from disdain to discovery. It was nourishing to find others like himself, often grappling with similar issues, and he was reevaluating his relationship with Gino, his boyfriend of seven years. To my concerned query, he assured me that, when and if the occasion arose, he would only practice safe sex.

"I value my health too much to take risks."

Alexander's level of self-acceptance had been rising steadily. His new lightness, his new accessibility to others and the loosening in his physical armature helped pave the way for a life-transforming experience. During the merriment of a big family event, an older male cousin pulled Alexander aside. Slightly inebriated and speaking from the heart, he gave Alexander an enormous gift: his realization of how difficult it must have been for Alexander to have grown up gay in a family that didn't acknowledge him. The cousin went on to apologize for his own lack of sensitivity.

"Listening to my cousin, hearing words I had never heard before—I felt so loved and accepted," he said, crying openly and freely.

Alexander subsequently dreamed of his conservatory teacher dressed not in her usual reserved teaching garb but wearing a flowing, diaphanous dress and moving freely. I asked what message she was bringing him in this dream.

"To be true to myself."

"What message would the other important women in your life want you to hear?" I queried.

"From Helga, to live life fully. From Ms. K., it was all about artistry."

"In other words, their collective wisdom tells you to bring all your selves together: Be true to yourself as a gay man, live life fully in the world at large, be your artistic self as a musician. Very smart women, these!" I exclaimed, enjoying my own interpretation, and wondering if, in the future, he would add a fourth older woman to the pantheon.

"Yes, all women," he said, as if this was the first time that fact had occurred to him. "I wonder why." He looked at me. I raised my eyebrows and turned my palm toward him, thrusting the question back. "They must be my feminine side that I've tried to hide. And the part tied to the music inside me. Hmmm. That's so interesting."

The Elusive Third Self

Alexander's views of himself as piano teacher and as a gay man were expanding, but insecurity still plagued the performing artist. I noticed that his breathing became shallow when he played, and I mused aloud whether not breathing fully was another way of hiding. Thinking this a terrific interpretation, I was immediately disabused of that notion by his answer: "Yeah. That sounds right." Tucked into his own thoughts, looking past me, he countered with, "If I play for you, I must be exceptional first."

His response caught me off guard and I muttered something about how concepts like "exceptional" and "perfect" distance us from actual experience.

Alexander nodded in reluctant agreement. He slowly placed the music to the Chopin *Prelude in C# Minor* before him on the piano, music he'd been carrying with him for weeks while avoiding bringing it over to the keyboard. That Prelude is short and fast, consisting of four phrases with cascades of descending notes in the right hand accompanied by ascending rolled chords in the left.

As he played, Alexander kept starting and stopping. "I get so upset when I'm playing and not liking what I'm hearing, and I can't change the sound as I play. So I stop. I'm having difficulty making connections between phrases." Making connections between phrases, I thought, was an apt metaphor for making connections between his selves. Pursuing connections between phrases would be one way of bridging the gap between selves.

"Let's take a very small section of a phrase and work for success with a few notes. Then you can add a few more."

He looked wistfully at the music as I spoke. "Taking things apart—that's so completely different from what I do at home, impatiently going over and over the same thing, trying one thing after another. Sometimes it comes out okay. But it never stays."

"That's like gambling," I responded, using one of my favorite expressions for ineffectual practicing. "Going over and over something that isn't working is like continuing to pull the lever on the slot machine hoping to see the three cherries pop up in a row." I repeated the oft-quoted phrase from my former teacher Alexander Libermann: "'Practice doesn't make perfect; it makes permanent.' That means, make sure to practice only what you want. Can I show you how to stop gambling, and practice for more predictability?"

I knew that question evoked conflict for Alexander, as it would entail allowing me, a musician-colleague, to guide him. His need to figure out musical problems independently, without relying on anyone else—especially not a colleague—had been a theme throughout our work together. I acknowledged how risky it must feel to reach for assistance. Independence was the family credo.

His answer, after a long, pensive silence, demonstrated the intensity of his inner dialogue. "It's an incredible gift, this opportunity to sit at the piano and be able to talk. I always thought things were hardwired, that my anxiety was like a plague. But I see myself changing all the time. And yet it's still hard to trust." More silence. I could almost hear him thinking.

Then, most soberly, he added: "What I think I need now is to go through pieces without stopping before we actually do the practical work of lessons. That's what feels right." He was calm and grounded. His speech held my attention in a new way.

Nodding assent, I rejoined, "Then that's what we'll do."

Practicing for Success

Over the next six months, Alexander and I spent most of our time together at the piano. Usually, he set the agenda by announcing his goal for the session. I attended to his agenda with curious expectancy. Though he was comfortable talking about emotions and doing exercises to promote ease, Alexander had continued difficulty overcoming his shame at not knowing exactly which steps were necessary to achieve his musical goals—hence, his ensuing reticence to permit me to be "teacher." Nevertheless, I was enthralled at the wisdom of his unconscious as it led us through myriad twists and turns to arrive at a place of peace. And always, there were surprises.

Here are highlights from those sessions, leading to the dramatic, if anticlimactic, ending.

At first Alexander found it crucial to revisit playing for me "just to experience what that's like. I don't know exactly why, but it feels very important that I play 'raw' in front of someone, not just by myself."

I knew that entailed my sitting and listening as an accepting, noncritical witness. Perhaps in doing so, I thought, he might exorcise "the devil between my fingers," as he had once described me as judge.

Alexander's goals then took on broader dimensions, allowing me to participate more. "I want to play two pages of the *Sarabande* [from Debussy's *Pour le Piano*] from memory. I want to see if I can let go of mental interruptions, and I want you to listen to see if it flows." He played almost to the end, reporting only slight mental interference. That was a major accomplishment in itself. But we did agree it didn't flow. I demurred from saying anything further. It had been enough at that moment to have been asked for and given musical feedback.

"I want to play through the Chopin *Prelude in C# Minor* again, this time without stopping." He did so. Knowing he might talk about all that he didn't like when he finished playing, I hastened to point out he had successfully met his goal by playing through without stopping. Predictably, he countered with, "But my mind froze while I played." I asked him to indicate the exact spot at which his mind froze. He did so, explaining it wasn't "because I couldn't play it, but because I suddenly thought, 'Am I going to get through without stopping?'" Would he be willing to apply the exercises he knew to alleviate mental interference? He quickly responded by taking a few moments to calm himself. At the mind-freezing spot, he practiced Sitting-in-the-Release after each note and listening intently to the sound of each note as it faded. Then we focused on the mind-freeze place and he played it with the same Sitting-in-the-Release care, starting with two bars before the spot, ending two bars after.

"This is so different from hard work," he said, with tears in his eyes. "It almost feels like a sin." Sadness followed and I enjoined him to sit with his feeling, just like Sitting-in-the-Release, without dissecting how he felt.

The following week, Alexander surprised me by declaring: "I noticed this week while I was practicing that I stop breathing during rests and when there are periods of quiet in the music." When I last observed to him that he didn't breathe fully and mused whether that was another way of hiding, he was not taken with my thought. Now he was noticing it himself, a much more powerful way to learn than being told! His statement shook me into my own free association: how breathing takes time, creates space for the person, gives him visibility, is fluid . . . Alexander's lack of fluidity . . . his often rigid outlook . . . his frequent lateness to sessions . . . and before I knew it, my thoughts took verbal form.

"Do you think there's a relation between your not breathing fully and the fact you are often late for sessions?"

His response showed remarkable insight. "Yes, there's definitely rigidity there. I decide how it should be and don't give myself extra breathing space. I decide how much time it should take to get here, and don't allow time for anything to interfere, like traffic or bad weather." He took a moment in reflection, eyes trained on the floor.

Slowly raising his head, he said: "I have a horror of calm—of arriving early and having to wait. Rests are very hard for me." A moment's silence. "That must be what's stopping the natural flow of movement. . . . This is very important. When I stop breathing I cut myself off from the music. I see the connection."

It was the another Chopin prelude, a stately gem in C minor with twelve bars of chords, that served as a pivotal moment in Alexander's striving to make connections. After playing this haunting Prelude, Alexander was displeased that the chords sounded disconnected from each other. He then accepted my offer to demonstrate how I would render the chords into long phrases. It won't surprise you, dear reader, to learn that the process involves feeling the music's continual movement within the body while arms and hands move rhythmically with one's breathing.

Alexander spent the rest of that session absorbed in creating the sensations we had explored. Afterward he announced, "It feels like being in water, like being afloat."

Another session: Alexander played the entire Debussy *Sarabande* without stopping, but reported that the sound of the very first note displeased him, immediately jolting him into his head and away from the music for the rest of the piece. While he engaged in a litany of self-criticism, I took the opportunity to grapple mentally with the power of sound to derail Alexander. His obsession with sound seemed to me excessive even for a musician, and strangely disconnected from the music. What was the underlying component? While thus ruminating, my attention was arrested by his words.

". . . depressing when I don't sound like I want . . . shit. . . ." That caught my ear—I'd never heard him swear before.

Before I could put a preliminary patina on my thoughts, I blurted out, "Is your need to sound perfect the same as your need to keep up a 'perfect' front to the world?"

He was very quiet before replying in a soft, wistful voice. "When I was twelve, I played with great passion—I didn't care about the sound, just about pouring my feelings into the piano." Alexander appeared to be stepping back into a moment from his past.

"Talk to me from where you are," I invited, moving slightly forward to encourage and support.

"Lonely and ashamed. I can see that twelve-year-old, but he can't look directly at me. He's turned sideways. This makes me incredibly sad. I want to help him play with a beautiful sound so he won't feel ashamed at not being good enough. The piano is the only place he can put all his feelings." Looking up, he added, "Lots of painful memories."

"So sound and passion need to find each other. How can you imagine connecting with your lonely twelve-year-old?"

Without answering, Alexander turned to the keyboard and played a few pages of his favorite Chopin Nocturne, then looked up with an enigmatic smile. "My twelve-year-old self is listening . . . but I can feel he's frightened, afraid I'll judge him."

"Play the Nocturne again, play it for him and send him the message that your sound needs to connect to his passion. You belong together." Alexander turned back to the piano and finished his Nocturne. Another connection was being forged. He looked somber as he left that day.

Alexander strode into my studio a few weeks later, on time, declaring, "I want to go through the Debussy *Sarabande* in a structured way, only working for success." I raised my eyebrows and smiled. He continued. "I'm going to set one small goal and you can help me figure out the practical ways to achieve it."

"Sounds good. What is that small goal?"

"To take the first four bars and really learn them." He played them but immediately fell back into anger with himself at disconnected phrasing.

I gently prodded: "Don't waste time with anger, Alexander. Ask the right questions: What didn't work and what do you need to get it better?" We reviewed the de-glitchifying process: analyzing what went wrong, how to solve it, calming oneself, then playing slowly and correctly while Sitting-in-the-Release.

"That feels wonderful," Alexander declared after tackling a glitch in the third bar. While searching for the right solution, he said he had this fleeting vision of himself "as a performing pianist, looking elegant just as I am." How sublime and delicious I found his juxtaposing elegance to the de-glitchifying process!

The next week Alexander walked in, exclaiming: "I was very excited this week when I practiced 'de-glitchifying' a single phrase. Instead of reprimanding myself for doing so little, I actually felt elated."

Alexander had always been thoughtful during his process of self-discovery, but now he was using everything as tools to foster understanding and growth. He gave a chuckle when he launched one session by saying, "I thought of you when I saw the movie *Prime*," which is about a therapist whose client is dating the therapist's son.

"Oh, are you dating one of my sons?" I asked with a grin and we laughed.

"Not exactly. It was more about you in the role of therapist. When I first came here I was very uncomfortable. . . . I saw you solely as a musician, yet I found myself telling you things I've never told anyone. When I look back at that time, I like the part of me that sat there," referring to the chairs in which we often sat away from the piano.

"That intelligent, analytic, thoughtful part?" I asked.

"Yes. But I've come to see that it's also the stubborn, self-conscious part."

"The part that says you should be able to play something perfectly the first time?"

"Exactly. Then when I got uncomfortable sitting here, revealing myself, I would go to the piano but that didn't feel right. It was like playing the *role* of pianist rather than really being one." Alexander sat quietly a few moments, hands folded in his lap. "And all those long tangents I went on at the beginning! I must have needed to validate myself by showing you how I got where I am."

His thoughtfulness about himself thrust me back into my own self-questioning. Had I trusted and embraced his process as fully as I should have? Had I in any way stymied it? What had been *my* glitches as he fought to cohere all his selves, at piano and couch? These reflections formed my response to Alexander. "It's interesting that you stayed with the work even though it made you uncomfortable." I knew this reflected my own discomfort.

"Yes, I think this all has to do with integrating the part of me that I like when I sit *here* with the part that wants so badly to be *there*, at the piano." As he continued discovering his personal truth, he was grappling with what exactly that meant. "Can I be honest and not feel exposed?"

"Yes. You can. You've freed yourself from hiding as a gay man, but you still have a choice when, where and to whom you reveal any part of yourself. You can tear down the walls that impede enjoyment of life, but keep those that protect you."

"Choices. I see." Then, he added: "I wonder how much of what I took as being honest was mere rationalization." Silence. "Oh boy, I'm really growing up here." His seriousness and lack of defensiveness was striking.

At the last session before the end of the year, we wished each other a Happy New Year. As he warmly hugged me, he added, "And that house in the hills I walked into," he said referring to his dream long ago of a house with light inside, "I know that was *this* house." He gazed around the room. "It is like magic coming here."

After the New Year break, Alexander began to prioritize his time commitments. Music was proclaimed top priority. He declared he was ready to look at the learning process from the beginning, slowly, thoughtfully.

After a few weeks of mindful lessons and practice, Alexander brought in a drawing he'd made. It was a circle with a triangle inside, the points of which touched the circle's circumference. He explained that the triangle's three points represented his three selves. The circle he imagined was made of diamonds and each of the triangle's points, red rubies. I was greatly moved as I contemplated his picture of precious stones, symbols of renewal. While we looked at the picture, he spoke about finally having to have *the* discussion with his father.

"When I think of wanting so badly to play, I think of how my father still can't recognize me for who I am. He doesn't understand either the musician or the gay me."

"Do you really think he doesn't know you're gay?" My question was received with pensive silence. I interrupted the silence. "I think there's a good chance he knows, and perhaps he's waiting for you to come to him."

The First to Know

The voice message was left at 11:30 on Friday morning, two days after our session.

"I wanted you to be the first to know. I just came out to my father and I also invited him to the party I'm having with a lot of my gay friends. This is a big turning point in my life. I'll see you next week."

I heard the tears in his voice. As I put the phone down, there was a lump in my throat.

It was a mature man who appeared at the next session. He related in great detail how he told his father about the party, which included his gay friends. "At the party he mingled freely. I caught sight of him several times chatting and laughing with different people. He seemed very at ease." Alexander sat back and breathed a huge sigh, his hands crossed on his lap, his countenance soft and serious.

"I'm a different person now," he claimed. After a few quiet moments in which Alexander looked around the room, and then out the window at the bare trees, he turned to me, saying, "I'm making a new friend and I decided I wanted to play for him as a means of letting him get to know me better. I want to make him that gift."

His music would be a gift now, not a hiding place. The words had been spoken so matter-of-factly it could have described something that often occurred. But Alexander and I realized how new such an occurrence was, and what a symbol it was of the changes taking place within his psyche.

It was not surprising, then, when Alexander decided he needed time off from our sessions. He needed, he said, to bring "order and integration" to his newly emerged and emerging self. I acknowledged the need with full support.

He eventually moved to a new apartment and lived alone. He supported himself with his piano teaching, a significant accomplishment. His studio thrived and he continued to be passionate about his music.

Postscript

Six months after our last session, Alexander sent me a note:

> *Last Saturday night I did what I have not done in a long time. I performed for a small group of very special friends, and I played from my heart. I can't believe I put myself in such an unpredictable position, for I had not prepared*

to perform. But I trusted my instincts. I was able to maintain composure and deal with the adjustments one needs to make as one performs. I thought of you a great deal. The work we did together was very present.

FIVE

THE STORIES AND MINDS OF ARIAH

The world of the grotesque is the darkness within us.[27]

— Haruki Murakami

"❝ I can't hear the music when I close my eyes."

Those were the first words I heard Ariah say. I had just given a presentation on Optimum Performance at a music teachers' convention and explained how my two professions of music teacher and psychotherapist impact each other. I had introduced the audience to a sensory awareness exercise geared toward enhancing concentration while listening to music, first with eyes open, then closed. Afterward, the audience posed some questions. That's when Ariah spoke.

I scanned the audience to locate the speaker. She was attractive, with flowing brown hair, somewhat heavyset and sitting in a wheelchair. Though she appeared to be in her twenties, her voice had the quality of a younger person. That, coupled with her physical condition and her statement, made me wonder what had happened to this woman to make her unable to hear music with her eyes closed. I was soon to learn and, in so doing, to reach the outermost limits of my own tolerance for emotional pain.

"Stories are the music of how the mind works," was a quote I'd jotted down during a lecture by Dr. Daniel Siegel, neurobiologist and author of *The Developing Mind*. If so, the phantasmagorical story I eventually heard from Ariah testified not only to the mind's complexity, but also to its capacity to create, store, obfuscate and illuminate memories that are the narrative of a person's life. Hers revealed a mind juggling the need for emotional survival with living in an environment she experienced as brutal. Ariah's story exemplified the mysteries of human nature, evil, and the will not only to survive but to live a meaningful life. It attested to the power of music in Ariah's quest for psychic reparation. She had chosen her name, pronounced Aria. It was her hunger for music amid her soul's darkness that led her to me.

After my presentation, Ariah asked if we could meet. I agreed, and the next day found us sitting together in the hotel lobby, she in her wheelchair, I on a cold, marble bench. Her words were gripping and, though spoken calmly, belied a sense of urgency. As I watched, listened and took mental notes, I saw her watching me intently, as well.

"Music is the most important thing in my life," she told me. "I cannot live without it. I once achieved a very high level of playing, even played a Beethoven concerto with a community orchestra in my teens. But now. . . . There has been a lot of abuse in my life." She paused and gave an ironic laugh. "More than a lot. It wasn't just the abuse at home of being told how awful I was, how stupid, how I could never amount to anything. When I practiced, I was told how awful I played—my father played piano himself. Certain pieces, like Bach's *Italian Concerto,* belonged to him exclusively. When I tried learning it, he would become ferocious, tearing into the room—I thought he was going to choke me." She looked directly at me. It felt as if she were scanning my face for a reaction. When our eyes caught and held for a moment, I kept my expression as neutral as possible.

In a tight, strangled voice, she continued. "But worse was the abuse from the group my parents belonged to. . . . I know it doesn't seem reasonable, but there were these people who believed in the weirdest things, and they needed little kids to participate . . . by hurting them . . . having sex with them . . . sometimes even . . . murdering . . . dismembering them. . . ." After a long pause she added: "They damaged my insides. I can't have children of my own now."

At this point Ariah stopped speaking and looked past me. She seemed to have retreated into herself, and I wondered if she was dissociating. Whether or not the events she described had actually occurred, it was clear she was in their thrall. A moment later she looked at me and, as I purposefully held her with my eyes as a means of prodding her back to the present, she did indeed reconnect.

A part of my mind was racing. I needed time to reflect. I wondered at her revealing this story to a stranger at first encounter. And I was grappling with incredulity about the story itself.

"I still get flashbacks. I see myself on the table where they placed the little girls before inserting things into us. They damaged me inside. They used blunt instruments, and they chanted as they did stuff to us. Often they wore masks, like devils, ghoulish faces. I . . . still get anxiety attacks, especially during Halloween. Seeing people in masks, I get confused and go back in my mind to those times." But," she added emphatically, "the worst part is I can't play the piano without breaking down in tears, or panicking. You see, abuse happened at the piano, even, with my mother, but . . . I can't talk about that." We were quiet again, and my private thoughts pulled me inward. Listening to Ariah's narrative was exhausting. I had no idea what to do next.

Ariah must have sensed this. She went into "persuasion" mode. "When I heard your lecture yesterday, I knew I had to work with you. I have had many piano teachers and many therapists, but you are the only person I've met who combines the two most important areas in my life." She stopped. "That's why I'm trying to get my story out as quickly as possible." Then she added, and for the first time I saw the semblance of a smile on her face: "Someday you'll write a book about me."

Decisions

Ariah's story challenged me on many levels; I needed time to sort it out. From a merely logistical standpoint, I foresaw several hurdles. She wanted to work with me but lived in a city more than an hour's drive from mine. She was in a wheelchair and there are several steps to my studio. Also, we would be dealing with highly charged issues, and I wondered who else closer to her home could provide support and immediate succor for Ariah if needed. How would our work dovetail with any other help she was receiving?

And finally, what to make of her story? I'd worked with abused, traumatized and dissociated clients before but had not been confronted with the magnitude of evil in her story. Where was the truth? How to distinguish reality from fantasy, and would that even be necessary to our work? Most important, I asked myself: Could I help her?

When we first met in the hotel lobby, I wondered about her judgment in revealing her history so openly and quickly to me, a stranger. Usually clients need time to establish trust with their therapist before revealing such traumatic material. Ariah provided the answer in a diary entry she wrote right after meeting me and that she later showed me:

> As soon as I heard and saw Margret I knew I had to work with her. It felt that important. She was the first person that brought the two halves of my life together and I instinctively knew I could trust her. If we did work together, I vowed I wouldn't run from the work, no matter what that entailed. And it was clear to me that day that I had to compel her to see me by being as open and honest as possible. Inside me the biggest struggle was going on, parts of me tugging to get me away from her, stop talking, run and hide. But I knew I had to stay present, tell my story. Even the hard parts.

In the following days, we spoke on the phone several times, exploring the possibility of working together and addressing the questions I had. She assured me of her local professional support and sent me letters authorizing me to speak with her internist, the psychiatrist who prescribed her meds and the social worker who acted as her therapist. I called each, explained who I was and asked questions. Each one expressed support for my working with Ariah and agreed to stay in contact with me. The doctor was just getting to know Ariah but stated she had multiple physical ailments among which was an autoimmune disease, probably lupus. She used the wheelchair on those occasions when she was in extreme pain, but normally could get around without it.

When I directly asked her social worker/therapist her thoughts about the veracity of Ariah's story, she sighed. "There's no way to know for sure. There have been similar reports from that geographical area, but who knows for certain? Ariah is definitely convinced. And she definitely suffers from trauma, flashbacks, panic, memory lapses. She has a history of dissociation, but appears mostly integrated these days. The truth almost doesn't matter. Something has left its awful mark on her and it's our job to help her move on now and make the most of her life."

I asked how she viewed my role with Ariah.

"You would bring music back in her life, you would be her cheering squad when things got difficult. She is strong. She is a brilliant, creative woman. You will be good for her."

I reviewed the literature and consulted with specialists in sexual abuse, cult abuse and dissociative behavior. If Ariah and I worked together, I would definitely need my own support system. There seemed to be agreement that there was no assured method to differentiate what had actually transpired from what a mind manufactures. But, no matter what the truth was, Ariah did indeed suffer real physical and emotional handicaps. I hoped her social worker was right—that I would be good for her.

Ariah and I agreed she would come for two ninety-minute sessions the following week, after which we would evaluate whether we should work together. We did meet, and we decided that, yes, we would work together.

And we did, for six years. At the end of that time we discussed fulfilling her prophecy about my writing a book about her. I thought we should each have a voice in the book. We thus embarked on a writing project that would illuminate her story from both our perspectives. This chapter is the result. I've assembled my part from the voluminous stack of notes I have of our sessions and from the many phone calls between Ariah and myself and with others concerning her. Ariah, in turn, contributed substantially from her writings in a diary she had kept for many years, and in which she wrote after our sessions. She told me she often forgot details, but could supply the much-needed emotional component to our project. In addition, she gave me her poetry, as well as letters written often to herself but also to her parents. Sometimes Ariah threw the unsent letters to her parents in a drawer; other times, she'd mail them, only to receive replies, which infuriated her. Ariah used writing therapeutically to help her through the darkness. She was an able, articulate scribe.

Toward the termination of our work together, Ariah handed me an amazing tape recording she made with a girlfriend who had known Ariah through her many years of trauma and dissociations. I listened to these two old friends reminiscing about their multiple adventures. Through tears and laughter, in which I often joined while listening, they recounted the sublime and absurd reality of Ariah's experience and its impact on her close friend. You will have a chance to read a transcript of that tape as well, after you know Ariah better. It has been a humbling and challenging experience to arrange our joint materials so that Ariah's story might be told.

Cages: The First Sessions

Ariah walked robustly into my studio. No wheelchair. She sat down and quietly announced that she had had a dream in which she performed. Remembering that she'd earlier declared how merely thinking of playing elicited fear and anxiety, the dream, coming at the start of our work together, seemed like an auspicious beginning.

"Well, then, some part of you has already made the leap and decided it's safe to perform. Can you draw a picture, without worrying what it looks like, that represents the process that got you there?" Without hesitating, she drew two pictures with crayons and pen.

The first picture was of a cage surrounded by heavy black bars with one side open. She wrote the word "piano" inside the cage in bold black letters. Outside the open door she wrote "hope" in yellow crayon. At the bottom she penned the words "fear of healing process."

The second picture looked as if it were drawn by a child. The page was colorfully decorated with flowers, hearts and ribbons, and the words "love & freedom w/ music" floated at the top of the page. She penned the words "fear mixed w/ hope" at the bottom. She was intensely involved while drawing, and looked to me like a youngster at school. Years later, when she read this chapter, Ariah concurred. "I remember the process of drawing. I did feel very young—probably about six."

When Ariah finished the drawings, she regarded them eagerly. As she had shown herself open to my suggestions, I continued by asking her to demonstrate the feeling each picture evoked for her by physically assuming statue-like poses of each picture in turn. Without pausing, she assumed the pose for picture #1 by shifting her left foot behind her, stating that it felt "stuck in cement." She poised her right foot in front, as if ready to march. Her right hand reached out "to the rest of my life," she declared.

Taking a stance to represent the floral picture was equally immediate. She simply raised both arms until they were completely outstretched, her face reflecting the optimistic stance her body had taken. I asked her to move slowly between her two stances, remaining aware of what it felt like to alternate between them: from "stuck-in-cement" to "moving-forward-into-life."

Her pictures provided me with the positive view of herself that suggested not only determination but also a capability of striding forward. Was this part of her persuasion mode to get me on board? If so, was it conscious or unconscious? Either way, it provided me with a view I would need during our sometimes tortuous work together: the view that she was passionately determined to get to "moving forward into life" and that she would explore any and all avenues to do so.

She pondered her pictures a few moments, and then put the drawing of the caged piano at one end of my studio and hesitantly took a few steps away from it. She stopped and said, "Without the cage it feels like I'm entering a foreign country." After a few moments I remarked that she had drawn the pictures from right to left, and wondered out loud if she could be Jewish, since Hebrew is written right to left. She nodded "yes," adding that she had gone to the Mikvah (a Jewish tradition of ritual cleansing, symbolizing the sanctity of sacred relationships) the previous night. Clearly, coming to her session with me was an event of moment in her mind.

Looking back at the caged piano picture lying on the floor, she stated in a vehement voice, "I want to tear that picture up. I want to move on, forget the past."

Perhaps, I mused, rather than destroying it, she could use the image to help her transition into her future. "Destroying the past destroys part of who you are, even if it's not a part you like. Can you imagine making something—anything you wish—out of the cage and piano image?"

She turned to me, smiling. "Yes, I can do that."

Without thinking, I blurted out: "You and the piano are innocent. You will need each other to heal." As the words reverberated in my head, I wasn't even sure they rang true. But Ariah had taken them in, as I was to read later in her journal.

Ariah left the session calm. But I was left mentally exhausted as I recalled all that had transpired in an hour and a half. I wondered how it would get translated within Ariah's psyche.

Several years later, she showed me this excerpt from her journal written after that first session.

I sat, my body erect, my mind racing: "Flee or fight—or is it fight or flight?" Either way, a decision needed to be made. The piano stretched before me, its eighty-eight keys reaching for my touch like a cat yearning to be pet [sic]. I looked down at my hands. My small fingers were curled into fists, and my knuckles were white with tension. "Breathe," a voice from behind reminded me. "Center yourself." I looked down from the ceiling and heard myself thinking, "Quick! Make a run for it!" But I didn't run. I had decided the moment I met Margret that if somehow I could work with her I would not run. That's what this was about after all—not running from my own mind, my emotions, my body, and most of all not running away from the music inside me.

When I finally saw her journal entries of this period, I was sorry not to have seen them while she was writing them, given her references to looking down at herself from the ceiling and being spoken to by a voice behind her. It would have given us the opportunity to discuss whether she'd been dissociating during our session, since it had not been apparent to me at the time.

What had been apparent was Ariah's resolve not to run away, including not running from the assignment I had suggested: that she reimagine, however she could, the cage she had both drawn and physically experienced as a stance that symbolically represented the cage. I was completely unprepared for what she brought to the next session.

What she brought was a small, square structure made of children's wooden blocks (see photo 1, opposite). Within the structure were strewn parts of mutilated dolls, "too broken to talk, beat up, numb," whispered Ariah. A severed head lay with eyes and mouth taped. Severed arms and legs ringed the structure; a spiderlike figure hung inside, an angel figure placed on top. This structure Ariah said represented where she'd been.

Fortunately, she had also created a structure of where she wanted to be.

This structure was a flat, carpeted piece of wood like a living room floor (see photo 2, opposite). At one end she put regular miniature living room furniture: a

PHOTO 1

PHOTO 2

couch, a rocking chair and a coffee table. They were joined by a child's fanciful objects: a bottle of bubbles, some candy-caned birthday cake candles. At the other end was a platform about two inches above the living room with a doll seated at a piano. A friendly turtle looked up at her from the living room floor.

My eyes were riveted by the offerings on the table before me: the devastating quality of the first structure juxtaposed with the hopefulness of the second. While time had felt fleeting during our first session with one activity segueing into another, time now stood breathlessly still.

Later, it would be Ariah who remembered specific details of that session. Mostly I remembered the stillness. I was glad I had not scheduled another session after seeing Ariah. I needed to remain in that silence while I contemplated the constructions of her past psychic mutilation and future hope.

After she left, I took the structures to my back porch, placed them carefully on the table and sat with them. I took pictures of them. A complex set of sensations overtook me: numbness, shock, sadness, foreboding and forlornness—presumably, the emotions that had accompanied Ariah throughout her life. How had she survived such a tidal wave of emotions? Then I became aware of the helplessness I was feeling. Was I picking up Ariah's own feeling of helplessness? Or were they mine as I contemplated her constructions? In fact, Ariah did not present as helpless—she was a fighter: Only someone with vitality and strength could have survived a life fraught with physical and emotional vicissitudes of such magnitude.

The following is her journal entry written while building her structures:

> *I came back with an assignment to make "however" the cage and the carpet. I went to the .98 cent store for most supplies and got the rest at Target.*

> *9:20 a.m.–10:40 a.m.*
> *I worked on the cage—designing it with blocks and starting to attach the blocks. I listened to storm and nature music in the background. Around 10:30 I had the thought that I was returning to the cage. I tried to remember the carpet or the safe place. I continued to get nervous . . . took Xanax and started writing.*
> *Yesterday when I went to the piano I was able to feel the way I felt on Margret's carpet . . . felt okay. Then in ten minutes I started panicking so I thanked*

the piano and I congratulated myself for the ten minutes. Then I sat for a while and looked at the piano and thought about the new concept that the piano was victimized too. I need to cleanse, renew, or transform it somehow. Too bad they don't have anything like a Mikvah for objects!

6:40 p.m.

Pretty much finished the cage. . . . Just making the cage was scary. I kept feeling guilty . . . then I reminded myself that I was making a representation of something painful, that I was not hurting myself or anyone else and that the purpose was for my healing.

Here is her journal description of her experience after her two sessions:

The . . . [sessions with Margret] have been quite telling in many ways— again. Monday I showed her the models—the cage and the ideal. She took photos. She not only asked how I felt looking at them, but how they felt looking at each other. The caged me couldn't talk, but managed a nod that she would like the other to play for her. We put the cage on the piano so she could see, hear, and even feel the vibrations. I played and sang "Child Inside." She wanted more. Next comes what was the most powerful part of all: I got out the Chopin E Minor Nocturne that I love so much but haven't been able to play decently. I played through 1 page, before I stopped—it didn't sound like I wanted it to. Margret had me move on to the second part of the first page and choose a point. I had to promise to play to that point and focus on playing to the girl in the cage. The girl in the cage wanted more. We went through the rest of the piece in segments like that—I became more relaxed and less judgmental and I was able to finish. Then Margret had me play the whole piece no matter what. I did it! I'm so proud and amazed!!

Ariah undertook these challenging exercises without hesitating, and her medical history helped explain why that was so, for included in that history were hospitalizations of varying lengths for depression, anxiety, PTSD (Post-Traumatic Stress Disorder) and DID (Dissociative Identity Disorder, formerly called Multiple

Personality Disorder). Her last hospitalization had been the year before our meeting. Treatment had occasionally included electroshock therapy. Because hospitals often include nonverbal treatment modalities such as art, journaling, music and movement therapies, Ariah undoubtedly would have experienced approaches like those, as well. Perhaps she had found them helpful, or at least not distressful.

Ariah and I had discussed her DID, and her many "alters." Alters are those dissociated parts of a person's identity that take on a life of their own. They have varying characteristics from each other and from the host, or primary person. Ariah named a few of her alters and gave a brief description of their roles. Little Laura functioned well in the outside world, but remained traumatized. Catherine came out when Ariah was nine. Catherine was the organizer who kept things together and got Ariah help when she needed it. She also led a good life, dating, meeting people, enjoying herself. Mollie stayed seven. There were the "kids" who watched *Sesame Street*; and there was Elizabeth, the creative problem-solver who took charge for two years when Ariah was seventeen. Elizabeth was a hard worker and got good grades. In time I would hear of others.

Ariah stated that over the years she had increasingly integrated her personalities into her "host" personality, Ariah—the primary person. Though her integration was not complete, she no longer found herself in strange or dangerous places without knowing how she got there. Here are some of the thoughts she sent me about dissociation, or "splitting," in her own words:

> *Dissociation from one's body is common—if not universal—among survivors of abuse. As the brain holds cognitive memory, the body holds somatic memories. Hidden memories in the mind and body color the way we treat ourselves and the way we interact with others. Post traumatic stress syndrome, eating disorders, depression, and sexual dysfunction are examples of the impact of unresolved issues surrounding past trauma. . . . Many people suffer their whole lives hiding from themselves. Those of us who are fortunate eventually come upon a situation where the preservation of a relationship with something or someone is important enough that we are willing to acknowledge, treat, and ultimately heal our hidden wounds. For me, the determining relationship was with the piano.*

The sense of fragmentation that Ariah experienced with alters was still being reflected in distinct and powerful psychic reactions. While she celebrated the conciliation made momentarily with her Chopin piece during the creation of her structures, she also wrote a long poem called "Screams Overtake Sounds," which included the following lines:

> *I sit and try*
> *to play in slow motion . . .*
> *Blood flows over ivory keys*
> *Screams overtake sounds*
> *Dare I attempt to find solace*
> *in Chopin?*

After receiving this poem, I once again wondered whether Ariah's story was not the concoction of a highly imaginative mind involving me in grand melodrama. But a stark mental jolt—or was it just reading that day's paper?—brought me back to the realities of evil. Could one doubt evil's existence, given what we know of humankind's use of torture, genocide and acts of depravity? Or deny how our culture reflects this shadow side of our souls in its books, plays, movies, art? Both fact and fiction testify to the dark, unsavory side of human nature. Was it that far-fetched to imagine that Ariah's story was true?

Herstory

When I saw Ariah after receiving this poem, we sat for long minutes in silence. She began speaking softly but with strength, anxious to fill in her story with more details, anxious that I know her better. Trauma and music remained the linchpins of that story. Her mother, she explained, was alternatively belligerent and seductive. With squeamish difficulty, Ariah related how her mother often sidled up to Ariah sitting on the piano bench to get Ariah to masturbate her. Other times she simply tore Ariah away from the instrument, angry at being reminded of her hated husband, whom she divorced when Ariah was five. Ariah sought refuge with her affectionate maternal grandmother who, however, suffered from manic depression and consequently also behaved erratically. But Ariah remembered her as the only one who told Ariah she loved her.

Ariah's father, an accomplished pianist, exposed her to music from an early age, and lessons began when she was six. At seventeen Ariah attended Interlochen Arts Academy, but only for a year. It was at that time that she was granted a court petition, which allowed her to leave home and become a ward of the state. The court ordered a trust set up for her, to be funded by both parents and managed by a court-appointed trustee. Ariah lived in three foster homes until she was eighteen, then became independent.

The next eight years were spent between sporadic enrollments in several colleges, hospitalizations for psychotic or suicidal behavior and, in her words, hiding from her abusers and the cult. She made her way to the Midwest where she somehow managed to earn a B.A. in criminal justice, worked odd jobs and, most important, started giving piano lessons to beginners.

The legacy of the Holocaust plagued this second-generation survivor, as well. Her Polish paternal grandfather had survived Auschwitz, she told me as she handed me copies of documents bearing his Nazi-assigned number. His son, Ariah's father, survived the war by being hidden by nuns. Here are excerpts of a poem she'd written about her grandfather.

> *N U M B E R 60495*
> *A black suitcase bears the name . . .*
> *"Israel" added by Nazis*
> *Black shoes molded into the shapes of your feet.*
> *Black striped garments branded with the same number as your body*
> *N u m b e r 60495*
>
> *Two and one-half years you lived in this earthly hell . . .*
> *What was so special about N u m b e r 60495 that you survived?*
> *I hate it that you were tortured*
> *I hate it even more that you survived.*
> *To be "special" within the gates of hell is hardly a privilege*
> *I know. . . .*

A strange déjà vu between generations stirs my memory
Black and white photos before my eyes
Brainwashed echoes screaming in my ears
And I want to resign myself to the mercy of the electric fence
Believing for a time that to end life now would end misery then.

Israel's suffering. The captivity of N u m b e r 60495. One with my own.

Ariah professed belief that her grandfather's soul had to have been gravely compromised for him to survive; that he must have colluded with the Nazis, succumbed to acting as a beast himself. That remained conjecture. But the "strange déjà vu between generations" was not. Much has been written about the psychodynamic transmission of trauma from one generation to the next[28] and scientists are now delving into the genetic transmission of trauma, as well.[29] Thinking about the role this part of Ariah's history played in her life reminded me of my own history as the daughter of a Polish Jewish father whose mother and sister perished in the Holocaust. As a protected only child, I never heard anyone discuss the War, the family losses, the genocide, Nazis, even the Germans. Yet my early childhood was surrounded with that legacy: how could it not be, in the post-War years in New York City, with its influx of immigrants, many with numbers on their arms and untold stories of suffering?

I never understood the recurring dream I had, perhaps when I was three, of being chased by men in uniform through dark streets. I'd wake in a cold sweat. The words that reverberated in my naive mind to place the dream were "somewhere in Eastern Europe." But I had no idea what that meant. I never heard a harsh word against the German people from my parents, but I grew up prejudiced against them nonetheless. And I didn't know how to frame it for myself.

After years of wondering how such symbols enter a young unconscious, I finally understood. Children "imbibe" their surrounding environment with the same facility with which they imbibe their baby food. Their senses, uncensored verbally or cognitively, register the sensations of their caregivers. When a child is surrounded by highly charged events such as the Holocaust that are not discussed, the memories of which are often repressed, the silence surrounding the events resonates in the child's psyche, like a bomb without detonation.

Had Ariah, like myself, incorporated the family's experience through the rippling intergenerational effect? Had that experience then been distorted by the limited capabilities of a child's understanding? Despite being too young to comprehend my father's fears of remaining in a Europe threatened by Nazis, I dreamed of fleeing them myself. Had Ariah's exposure to her own family's torment turned into nightmares of herself as torture victim? A guilty survivor who should have felt the mercy of the electric fence? Or as someone who could erase the nightmare simply by not being? Did Nazis become satanic cult abusers in her child's mind? Would that explain dreams she wrote about in her diary, but only showed to me after we ended our work, and even then, with great trepidation?

I was at a music school and the cult sent someone to kidnap me. They caught me. Brought me into a gym room, left the door open, did sort of an exam, spit on my vagina, lit a match, and tossed it in.

There was also some sort of wedding ceremony where they put blood on my face and made me drink some sort of drug. We were all in a circle and all brides. I was supposed to maintain a certain physical position but couldn't. That told them I was "special." I ran away, even though I was terribly sore inside. I knew there wasn't much time. I was running around screaming out to others. . . . And then I awoke.

Trauma, inextricably interwoven with music. And always the fear of punishment, the perpetual accompaniment to Holocaust stories and childhood abuse. Never knowing when the blow will come, nor what provoked it, the survivor's psyche becomes habituated to its constant possibility. And, as with PTSD victims, any cue, no matter how subtle—a noise, someone breathing, music—has the power to provoke anxiety that a dreaded event will follow.

It was becoming clear that the role I would play in the large picture that was Ariah's life would center on the part of her trauma whose focal point was the piano. The therapeutic framework I provided gave her the freedom for verbal and musical expression while I endeavored to detoxify her relation to music and empower her as pianist. It would be delicate as well as challenging, for Ariah still had a therapist *and* a piano teacher.

"What part do *you* have in all this?" she asked me.

"I'm the catalyst for you to find your way back to your music."

She smiled. "I like that."

Clearly I was going to stay the course.

Ariah asked me, based on her past therapy experience: "If I ask you what you think about something, will you ask me back what *I* think?" I smiled, having experienced similar frustration when not getting an answer from my own therapist. But Ariah wasn't smiling.

"I will do my best, Ariah, to give you straight answers. I'll undoubtedly also want to know what you *do* think!" Then she smiled.

Ariah was a fierce fighter for her own health and often came up with unique ideas. Having been categorized by medical and psychiatric professionals for years with "every diagnostic label you can think of," as she remarked, she decided "diagnostic professionals need to add a category for artists and musicians": the Artistic Personality! Ariah was playing with ideas to help her feel better about herself and the intensity with which she experienced life. I applauded her for bringing her artistic personality to the forefront, thereby allying herself with people who have a developed sensitivity not only to external sensory input, but also to their own richly endowed internal world.

It was four months into our work. Ariah wished to make goals for herself, and came in with a "Master Plan with Backup." The plan included taking piano lessons consistently; setting dates for performing; finding a duet partner; and building up her own teaching studio.

Two days later she called me to say that one of her alters, her "little girl," had come out and "called" *her*. I tried imagining how an alter could make a call to the host, but stifled that thought to listen fully and take notes. The little girl told Ariah she was scared of getting into trouble for playing the piano. Ariah told me it wasn't like the old times when she'd split when an alter appeared. This time she was conscious of her alter speaking, but she mentioned being embarrassed by this younger person.

"No reason to be embarrassed," I blurted out. "It's better for the little one to be heard consciously than to ignore her and have her go underground again . . . so to speak." I wondered if that was making sense to Ariah in the context of her own experience.

We both noticed how quickly, after setting up music goals, the "little girl" got frightened. It took me a while to realize that every step forward provoked fear of punishment, and often two steps back.

One month later Ariah brought in the first movement of the Mozart *A-Major Sonata, K. 331.* Ariah proved to be very musical, and I honored the work she was doing with her regular piano teacher. Since our work focused on giving Ariah ways of alleviating panic at the keyboard and playing with ease, our work did not conflict with those ongoing piano lessons.

Ariah was already familiar with the principles from my book *Passionate Practice,* so it was natural to begin there. We practiced the calming and weight-releasing exercises to alleviate anxiety, and, as I often do, I audibly and slowly breathed alongside her in order to model and accompany her in the exercise.

Ariah went through the exercise with the Mozart Sonata on the music rack. As she cued herself to breathing easily, her body visibly relaxed. I gently lifted her arms from underneath. As she continued breathing I could feel the increasing weight in her arms. I asked her if she felt the weight in her arms. "No," she said, "I don't feel anything at all."

Though it momentarily surprised me, I quickly reminded myself of how difficult it often is, after a lifetime of living with tension, to make the transition to ease. With trauma victims who are particularly disconnected from their bodies, making the transition is doubly challenging. But we had planted the seed for the future.

I was pleased that Ariah had taken the step toward realizing her goal of moving from the couch toward the piano. Yet even as we knew the direction in which we were headed, we had to acknowledge that it entailed a constant shifting between the emotional and the musical, whether she was at the piano or not. We discussed this at great length. Then Ariah discussed this with her piano teacher at equally great length. And then, all three of us discussed it together and we concurred that it might be better for Ariah to take a break from her lessons during the time she worked with me. Ariah's teacher seemed relieved, as she quickly gave her wholehearted support to the plan. She undoubtedly had had her own challenging moments with Ariah that did not fall under the purview of normal piano lessons. I, too, felt relief because of the freedom I now felt to work on all aspects of the musical process.

Ariah graphically summed up her own view in a diary entry:

> *Before beginning my therapeutic work with Margret I lived outside of my body most of the time . . . mostly the line of communication between my brain and my body was disconnected. The times I did feel something I was actually feeling memories of things past—not in the present. I felt hands, lips, tongues, body parts that had invaded me years before. I choked on an erect penis and cried out from vaginal pain. I felt what I could not afford to feel then. Dealing with these somatic episodes was the focus of my therapy for years. . . .*

After writing about our work of breathing and releasing at the piano, she continued:

> *Margret wanted me to take deep breaths to help me relax. I remember her sighing as an example. I was terrified on two counts: I was afraid of what I might feel if I relaxed, and I was afraid of Margret herself. The latter is difficult to explain. It just felt to me that breathing was a private thing to do and it scared me to witness it. Still, I was able to stick to my resolve to trust this woman and do whatever it took to heal. As I took a couple of deep breaths I began to feel my body. Strange. Foreign. Healthy? Terrifying.*

A few weeks later I received a surprising call from Ariah. In a matter-of-fact voice she reported that she had hospitalized herself for suicidal depression for which she had just finished receiving electroshock therapy (or ECT). She sounded stable but was suffering from the memory loss that often accompanies this treatment. She told me that after the electroshock she'd begun getting a regular night's sleep. She spoke of the "models" she'd made in the first week of our work. She spoke about walking around my studio. But she didn't remember who I was.

"I found your name written on a paper in my desk. I wanted to make sure to make contact, if you are someone important in my life."

I sat there numb. The myth of Sisyphus came to mind, feeling as if we had just tumbled back down the mountain after strenuously pushing our individual boulders up a few inches. In a flash, I recalled my thoughts upon first meeting Ariah and embarking on our work together. I had sensed then that it would be difficult, emotionally taxing in ways I could not foresee.

Now I was discovering another essential part of the challenge: that after making strides forward, fighting demons and moving closer to achieving her goal of playing her beloved instrument, there could suddenly be erasure, and there would be no way of knowing what part of our work together would disappear and what part remain.

After our phone call, I sat staring into space. I tried to feel what it was like to have essential parts of my life erased from awareness. I could not. But then I turned to the other feeling I was experiencing: of *my* having been erased by her. That was scary. In addition to falling down the mountain together, I was being expunged from the entire experience. In the poignancy of the moment, I forgot what I knew of the effects of ECT, how the important threads in a person's life usually return. And of course I wasn't remembering Ariah's determination to make our work successful. At a visceral level I was experiencing Ariah's fateful path, which consisted of continual cycles, and I would need to remind myself of that almost as often as I needed to remind her, in her darkest moments, that "You have weathered many trying times; you have the strength to weather this one. Life is cyclical. You will bounce back."

Several weeks after her hospitalization, and many calls and repeated talks later, she came back "to be at the piano with you." She was sad about the time lost, sad that she still felt "caged." Ariah began crying over her childhood of abuse, over the children with whom she'd been abused, over the fact that she would not be able to have her own children.

"You are in mourning, Ariah." She nodded in agreement.

After a few moments, I asked: "Can you bring your mourning and sit with it at the piano?" She nodded again. We moved to the piano. After a few moments I asked her if I could lift her arm, and she nodded "yes." As I did so I asked her to be aware of her breathing. She breathed easily as I lifted her arm, and I could feel the weight being released from her shoulder into her arm, which was getting heavy.

She denied feeling any difference.

"I wonder if there's a place where you disconnect?"

She immediately responded, "The space between the shoulder bone and the arm bone," she replied, looking ahead at the piano. "Nothing's connecting."

I continued holding her arm up with my hand. "Can you find a way to gently, carefully connect so that energy flows freely in that spot?"

She smiled and said she just got an image of her teddy bear's arm, with its easy swing. Then suddenly, there was a surge of weight dropping into her arm like a torrent released from an opened valve. It was so precipitous that we both registered the shock of something momentous having happened.

Ariah burst into tears. She sobbed a long time before looking up and saying, "I haven't been inside my body for so long—I got very frightened when the connection was just made and I actually felt it." I watched her closely as her face, despite tears, appeared fuller, her body more grounded. It was exhilarating to witness such movement, but as before, when progress was made at the piano, some part of her retreated.

Later that day she left a message. "I'm calling to tell someone I'm really miserable—I'm telling you so I won't feel so alone. So I've told you. You don't need to call back."

I did call back and we discussed the tremendous issue of her getting "back" into her body. For the next few lessons we were careful in combining exercises that would keep her connected to and in her body, while forestalling anxiety. I interspersed moments of her playing with reminders to breathe and with questions to keep her present: "What do you see? What do you hear? How do the piano keys feel?

The phone message after one such lesson was decidedly more encouraging: "I got it! I felt my body *and* I could play at the same time. Thank you."

Improvising

The crucial issue of Ariah's connecting her arm to the rest of her body had been momentarily achieved. But it was a complex blessing, since Ariah's sense of her history dictated that punishment follow achievement. It was not as strange as it sounds for Ariah to ask me, "Are you going to disappear?" She needed reassurance that finding ease at the piano would not elicit punishment from me by abandoning her.

Ariah progressed and practiced at home without succumbing to panic, and was happy when the new techniques gave her mastery over previously difficult passages. At the same time she grappled with her overall condition: the constant adjustments of her many medications, huge mood fluctuations and all the people she relied on in her life for support. Her list of medications was staggering. A partial list included meds to help correct her hormonal imbalance from the hysterectomy she'd had early in life, plus antidepressants and antipsychotic drugs, despite the fact that her psychiatrist had told me he didn't think she was psychotic. One drug often interfered with another, necessitating more tweaking.

I spoke with her social worker after some particularly depressed phone calls with Ariah. "No one really knows what's going on," she admitted, and once again concurred that it was important that I hold the positive "valence" for Ariah—it was something no one else was in a position to do, focusing, as each provider did, on a circumscribed aspect of her illness. Holding a holistic view of Ariah coincided with my natural inclination. I perceived a woman with talents, intelligence and plenty of strength to meet the inordinate medical and psychological challenges she faced. Regarding her as a whole, unique individual engendered hope, as did the quote from Nietzsche that Ariah included in her teaching brochure: "Without music, life would be a mistake." Music for Ariah had been the single most sustaining factor in her life.

And yes, Ariah had a growing teaching studio. She and I sat back to contemplate how far she had come from panic and fear at the piano to writing and printing a brochure for her studio. Ariah loved teaching, nurturing children, and being patient while they learned at their own pace. She had an abundance of patience, having had to cultivate a bottomless reserve for herself.

By our second year I was (finally) used to the shape of progress Ariah crafted, like an underground animal burrowing ahead, avoiding barriers, crawling sideways, backward, sitting immobile to avoid attacks, yet always veering in the desired direction. It was hard to pinpoint phases in the work, for the legacy of Ariah's physical and emotional history perpetuated the cyclical process of progress. I continually improvised to keep up as she herself steered her course.

Ariah came to one lesson sighing. She had had an exhausting session a few days before with her social worker, which stirred up upsetting details of her abuse by her mother. Ariah reported that when as a child she played well, the abuse became worse. As she spoke, her agitation was palpable. I knew her well enough to know that talking about it would not be productive. I steered her to the piano and suggested that she improvise—something I knew she enjoyed—and, while improvising, verbalize her experience. She immediately took up the suggestion.

"Neat. This is the first time I've spoken while improvising. I'll call it 'Transformation in G Major.'"

And, just like that, we'd created a new therapeutic tool for ourselves: free association to free improvisation. Would that it could lead to a double freeing!

Ariah played simple major chords. "This feels great. Free. I can play and not worry about mistakes. But . . . what will happen to me if I do . . . ?" The music shifted to minor, slow and sorrowful. "I can't play. I'll get punished. They won't like it. . . ." More mourning music. "Well, I'm going to do it anyway," she declared with a loud series of chords, and returned to G-Major chords triumphantly.

Improvisation proved a worthy friend for Ariah. A bleak period followed the summer of our third year together: Her latest talk therapist had died. Ariah became paranoid, and her voices returned. I asked what her primary voice was telling her. She looked at me as if she were diving down inside herself to listen, then surprised me by saying, "It's telling me I need to be flexible in the way I set my life up so everything doesn't fall apart when one thing goes wrong." She wanted us to improvise together on the two pianos I then had in my studio.

"Improvising helps with my voices—it externalizes them. Maybe this will lessen their grip," she mused aloud. Afterward she related that "I feel very supported when you improvise with me, when you imitate what I've just played. And then, when you stopped playing and just let me play, it felt like you were letting me 'speak' through my music, without interrupting me. I liked that." Improvising at lessons, Ariah revealed, felt good because "I'm not alone; there's no right or wrong; there's nothing I have to work on later; no need to watch the details."

A Roller-Coaster Life:
Despair, Frustration, and Bumpy Triumphs

Ariah's musical life reflected the realities of the rest of her life. I have never ridden a roller coaster, yet the thought of it described my sense of Ariah's life. I marveled at her ability to remain on the ride, even get back on when it threw her.

It was the summer of our third year together. Summers were difficult for Ariah. The heat affected her painfully. At such times she couldn't leave her apartment, so we would work long-distance, phones held between necks and shoulders in those pre-cell days, each of us at our respective pianos. Fall's cool weather revived her, as it did her studio. Her reputation as a sensitive and creative piano teacher attracted young students, some of whom had emotional and physical challenges.

"I have this seven-year-old boy who is sort of autistic," she once remarked. "His mother cried when I said I'd take him as a student, since other teachers had refused. Whenever I get stuck, I think to myself, 'What would Margret do?' Then I do it. His mother thinks I'm wonderful."

Prior to a lesson with me, Ariah had a dream. "I dreamed I was an adult but living in the apartment where I grew up. First I dreamed that my dad came into my room and was molesting me. Somehow I had the piano in my bedroom. I basically kicked my dad out of the room, saying, 'I can't deal with this right now—I have to practice.'" She looked at me, adding, "It's humorous in a sick kind of way."

It was a positive sign that, instead of waking up in a panic and needing a tranquilizer, she booted her demon out of her dream. But if her emotional past was loosening its stranglehold, she still faced the realities of her physical illnesses, which at that time included "diagnoses of bipolar with psychotic episodes" and "an 'overlap' syndrome of MS, lupus and chronic fatigue syndrome."

"Retaining your sense of humor, sick or not, will help a lot," I said.

Ariah's sessions with me were paid for by a well-known musician in our area who had known Ariah since she was a child and believed in her musical ability and strength. He himself was a busy performer and teacher, yet he faithfully, graciously, supported Ariah's music lessons, recognizing beauty in a kindred (if wounded) spirit. Knowing this often helped me when my own belief in our work momentarily floundered: Ariah, like Tchaikovsky, had a patron!

Ariah could no longer postpone returning to her old love, the Mozart *D-Minor Piano Concerto, K. 466*. More and more, our sessions were looking like piano lessons.

Buoyed by this accretion of positive experiences and increasing energy, Ariah decided to return to school to become a music therapist. I was touched when she showed me her statement of purpose:

Music has always been my lifeline. [As a child] when I did not have the refuge of piano lessons, I buried the memories [of abuse] along with the piano. . . . In College, reunion with the piano was also my reunion with my suffering. Symptoms of post traumatic stress disorder permeated my lessons. Try as I may, I made very little progress. Then I met Margret Elson. . . . Finally, instead of trying to shield my teacher from my trauma, I was able to work through it. Together we excavated the piano from the memories. Music is once again a joyful, integral part of my life. . . .

When talking about going back to school brought up old feelings, Ariah brought me a picture album her mother had kept of her from birth. There was nothing particularly extraordinary about the pictures: mother and daughter together, occasionally a man standing nearby, a house, a park. To the outsider, a normal family album. Not to Ariah, who cried as she commented: "Sometimes there were these moments of just being together. Those were moments I always prayed would last. But then . . . well . . . I'm very sad," she said, as if she had to explain.

Once again, I returned to the theme of mourning. "You are going through mourning—for your childhood and all those awful memories." Silence. "There's no mourning without sadness." I paused, "Or then we'd have professional mourners." I stopped and thought. "Of course, they do have that in some societies," I added. Our eyes caught, and she flashed a smile.

"I could make a fortune!" she immediately retorted. Though still weepy, she managed to laugh with me. I asked her if she wanted to stay with the album and talk about it.

"No. You know the story. I just need to sit with the sadness for now." We sat together quietly, as we often did.

She suddenly shifted gears, closed the album and angrily said, "But I'm really angry, and not at my parents this time! My psychiatrist is taking a vacation, and I don't like the person I'd have to see instead. It makes me *so* angry when this happens." Her anger quickly turned to tears. I took note of this sudden shift from anger to tears. It seemed as if, rather than acting as a release valve, her crying suppressed the riskier emotion of anger. I asked Ariah what would happen if she didn't cry when she was angry.

"I'm afraid I'll split. That would be dangerous—I might smash things, take an overdose. I have plenty of meds around!"

"What if you stayed with your anger?"

"I'd burn in hell."

"Realistically speaking, Ariah, what would happen?" A few seconds of silence.

"I don't know."

"What if you went to the piano?"

She smiled. "That's exactly what I tell my autistic student when he gets frustrated." She took a thoughtful moment. "But, if I went to the piano and only practiced, it would feel like stuffing my emotions back."

"Well then, what else could you do?" She smiled, looked around, then answered by devising an alternative to playing: When intense emotions arose, she would first improvise—which allowed her to let her emotions out—and *then* play the Mozart, which would be using the feelings productively. Another momentary breath of fresh air was injected into an old behavioral reflex. For now, however, she needed to practice the first movement of her favorite concerto, which she would be playing at my upcoming student workshop. Despite the informality of my workshops, I would not let her play unprepared.

At the workshop, Ariah played her Mozart concerto, and I played the orchestra reduction on the second piano. Though her performance disappointed her, her diary entry shows how her thoughts about performing were evolving:

> I was able to see the good: Even though I was exhausted, I had played in front of people. Stage fright had been minimal, and in all fairness I had played well. In fact, I actually enjoyed myself. When I heard myself make sounds I didn't like, I could hear voices telling me I'm no good, but I was able to say, "Go away. I'm playing now."

As the third year rolled into the fourth, Ariah worked relentlessly to maintain what she had accomplished musically. But, once again, the roller coaster plummeted. At home when she practiced, she was often tormented with flashbacks, and in my studio when we worked on proper hand technique, fears of her hands being cut off emerged.

With difficulty she garnered the strength to tell me that "When you tell me what to do with my hands, it conjures up the times my parents told me what to do with them. . . ." She gulped for air ". . . to touch them . . . especially my mother . . . it felt awful . . . sticky. . . . I felt like a whore. Even now I feel like that telling this to you . . . such shame, want to disappear. . . ." Other times, she'd be drawn to playing Bach's Italian Concerto and would hear her father screaming at her, enraged for playing *his* piece.

As she spoke, I inwardly cringed. I wanted to scream over her words "STOP. This can't have happened. And besides, I don't believe it. Yes, I do. No, I don't. Yes. Yes. Noo." Would I rather have contemplated that the woman in front of me was completely out of touch with reality *and* melodramatic as hell, or that the woman in front of me was telling the truth? Both choices were repugnant.

As Ariah struggled to let the words out, she suddenly looked up at me with what I understood as a plea.

"Should I say those words?" I asked.

She nodded, yes.

"I will not stop seeing you because of anything you tell me. You are not a whore. And I'm not judging you." I paused. "But I do judge the adults who did these terrible things to you. I judge them very harshly."

After that day, the roller coaster plummeted yet further as Ariah went through another dark period. She had started to question the circumstances and reality of her abuse, the defining feature of her life. She came perilously close to a psychotic break, unable to distinguish between what was real and what was not. She was back in the hospital.

I urged her to keep a detailed, written account of our work so she could pick up the thread more easily when she returned. To keep connected through this forced separation, she took a picture of me. In a philosophical tone she quipped: "Other than being miserable, I'm okay." Then: "Tell me about how I am after ECT. It feels like the end of the line for me now."

Dutifully, and truthfully, I told her: "By observation and by report, ECT helps you regain your balance. For a while you experience memory loss, but you are less depressed and more productive after the treatments. Remember, life is cyclical and you always rebound." We arranged for her to call me on a certain day after her treatment in the hospital.

"You sound lucid now. And you remembered to call," I told her on the phone.

"I put Post-its all over," she replied. She was plagued by questions: Was she truly abused? Were her memories due to psychosis? Meds? At least, listening to music soothed her during this tormenting time. I suggested writing a big sign to put up over her desk, to read: "Yes, I'll get through this. I've done it before."

She laughed with contentment at our having had a nice conversation, one that she could actually follow.

"Yes, you were very present," I assured her.

"It's nice to talk with someone who really knows me."

"We have history."

When I spoke with Ariah's doctors, they told me that her "morphing" from one persona to another had frustrated the medical people, too. No sooner was something fixed with one personality than something else—like a skin rash—appeared. Did she have lupus? Multiple sclerosis? I queried. It's not clear, was their answer. And the work I do with her? Their reply: It is important work. It validates her without denying the issues. One doctor sighed, saying, "I wish we had more answers." So did we all, as Ariah underwent severe emotional and physical cycling.

In the fall of our fourth year, Ariah experienced a severe lack of motivation. She became terrified that not wanting to do anything would lead to her "disappearing." In her journal she wrote:

> When I am alone [without a witness] I am afraid that the emotions might be too strong and that I will simply burst into millions of pieces and be blown away into nothingness.

As we saw in chapter 3 with Celeste, who feared that her body parts would fly apart, making her disappear, the fear of disappearing is pervasive among people who have been abused. The activities that helped Ariah keep from disappearing were playing the piano, talking out loud and yelling at herself.

Serving again as her memory, I reminded her how she always went through cycles, and that, despite being in a down cycle, she had won some small victories, including not freaking out or having flashbacks during Halloween, and that it had not been necessary to hospitalize her for her most recent ECT, but that she had been treated as an outpatient. Every victory counts.

After this latest ECT, Ariah regained the Mozart, but the Bach *Prelude* we had recently begun disappeared.

She wrote the following in her journal:

What depression feels like to me:

Life is painstakingly difficult . . . what plagues me most is grief: grief over what should have been but never was. . . . I am always trying to rebuild my life somehow—rebuild a sense of identity, family, community, health, purpose. . . . I remember a time when my faith was strong. . . . What if faith is a product of the imagination and there really isn't anything beyond what I can see and touch? I know what it would take to end this. . . . Will taking away my body take away the feelings? Will I end up floating around trying to find a new body?

When I'm in this dark place, remembering healthier times doesn't help. Just because things were better once doesn't mean they will be again. In addition, no matter how hard I try I cannot re-create those good feelings inside myself. I wonder if they ever really existed. I do things that make me feel better: baths, music, friends, walks . . . and all that happens is that I wish everything would just stop.

I wrote to her during one bleak episode:

So how was today? I hope somewhat better. Your dark period has been too prolonged and it sounds like you are being tried like Job, big time. BUT SUICIDE IS NOT AN OPTION. It definitely is not your answer. The other things you mentioned are—concentrating and making contact with FRIENDS, music, prayer, flowers—SMELL them, if they don't give you allergies! And keep writing. Crying is okay too. But less okay than the other activities.

Slowly the machinery of Ariah's internal roller coaster would crank, gears noisily grinding, and the cars slowly begin the ascent. She wrote in her diary:

> *Despair appears to be coming to an end. Is it the changes in medication—*
> *off the heavy pain pills, and on a new anti-depressant, or would I have cycled*
> *out of it on my own? I'll never know. Bi-polar disorder remains a mystery to*
> *me. Mostly I have depression, and when I am manic, I don't get euphoric. I get*
> *bad insomnia and OCD kicks in. I cannot truly differentiate between OCD and*
> *mania. Oh, well, as I say with my physical illnesses—I don't care what you call*
> *them; I just want to get them under control, or better yet, make them disappear!*

Despite pain, insomnia and OCD—Obsessive Compulsive Disorder—Ariah returned to our lessons, and to her own teaching.

> *As much as I am beginning to feel like a real teacher, I miss being the stu-*
> *dent I once was. I'll probably never have those luxuries again—of weekly les-*
> *sons, regular practice. I want out of this cage. I guess I have to be patient.*
> *Damn. With Margret I prayed and played my way through terror, rage, pain. I*
> *wrote and cried; danced and cried; drew pictures and cried; talked and cried;*
> *developed artwork and cried. Cried and shivered and sobbed . . . cleansing*
> *myself from the inside out. I haven't been a very good student, but I am blos-*
> *soming into a wondrous teacher. Now it's my turn to do the watering, feeding*
> *and nurturing of my students.*

Ariah was blossoming as a piano teacher. Even during her most trying periods when our sessions were intermittent, she called me for consultations on musical and pedagogical issues. With a student about to play in an upcoming music teachers' competition, we once again took up our separate stances at our respective pianos, phones cradled between ear and neck, and worked out the ornamentation for a Bach piece and the fingering for a passage in a Chopin Nocturne.

An incident with one of her new adult students revealed Ariah's true calling to herself. Using ideas from *Passionate Practice*, Ariah guided her student through the "Calming Light" and "Sitting-in-the-Release" exercises. Afterward, the student massaged her hands and said she felt them healing. Then she cried as she told

Ariah the story of having tended her sister as she lay fighting for her life after surgery, grasping her sister, gripping the ends of the sheet to help move her, and, as Ariah wrote, "goodness knows what else she was holding onto so tight. She had never connected the pain she was having in her hands with that tight hold and now, with the exercises, she said she could 'let go.'"

She looked at Ariah through tears and called her a "Music Healer."

The role of music healer exhilarated and frightened Ariah. "Because of all the work we've done, I'm super-sensitive to extramusical issues," she told me. "The responsibility scares me. What if I get a *me*? Someone who feels the weight drop in their arm and hasn't been in their body for twenty-five years and starts to cry?"

"What would you do?" I asked, smiling broadly.

"Well . . . I'd say, 'It's a common thing to release emotions after not feeling them for so long. That can happen when you breathe through your body. . . .' Then I'd ask what they're experiencing, and, depending on the response, help them feel their body without fear or pain. When I trust myself I do the right thing, even when the issues are complicated." Ariah leaned back, her face and bearing at peace, like that of a music healer.

During this "up" period, she started her master's program. Having changed her mind about pursuing music therapy, she was now studying clinical psychology in order to become a licensed Marriage and Family Therapist—the degree and license I have.

At our lessons, Ariah worked intensely, as if trying to make up for lost time at the piano. She went back to Bach's *Prelude in E Major* from Book I of the Well-Tempered Clavier. I demonstrated playing Bach expressively, remaining faithful to Baroque style. When Ariah was frustrated at not practicing for several days, she "consulted her piano," a technique in *Passionate Practice* that encourages dialoguing with one's instrument. She recorded their exchange:

Piano to Ariah: Fear is your problem, it exhausts you and you have more work to do. When was the last time you expressed any emotion—other than frustration—when you played me?

Ariah: True. It has been a long time. What has happened?

P: Somewhere along the line you checked out again. You found that you could relax the body by leaving it. That's part of why you have reverted back to your old technique of 'playing with your fingers.' At one lesson you started to get in touch again, but Margret told you not to cry. You didn't but that really fright-ened you and you haven't been in touch with me since.

A: So what do I need to do?

P: You have taken the first step by talking with me. . . . You are fearful and depressed and need help internally and externally. You need to adjust your psych meds—they aren't working. Also, learn shorter, simpler pieces.

To me she said, "This exercise reminded me of options I have and not to despair."

Indeed, it gave me food for thought as well, especially as it related to her cry-ing. It seemed that I had not understood the function that crying played for her: I needed to hear from her piano, no less, that her crying was not only productive, but even necessary in her ongoing battle for wholeness. Crying was not a distraction, but rather another physical act, like dropping weight into her arm, that helped her get into her body. Had I understood this earlier, I might have been able to help her use crying as part of the integrative process.

The "crying" issue was, however, slowly being metabolized in Ariah's system. A few days later she wrote in her journal:

> *Yesterday I talked with Margret about the crying when I play. I identified that it has both old and new qualities to it. The old qualities are: overwhelmed and melancholy. The new qualities are: openness, excitement, joy and hope. . . .*

Then, I received this email from her:

Dear Margret,

You don't know me directly, but I know you. I am part of Ariah. I hope she doesn't get mad at me for writing to you. . . . I need to tell safe people how alone I feel being separate again. I'm starting with you. The therapist and doctor know too. I am about 12 and I have a lot to do with the music, past and present. I am taking your advice, though, and learning to play through the tears. It's scary, but it works in that I get to keep playing, and without that I'd be nothing. I'm a little fearful that you will not understand me, and Ariah is a little fearful that because she split you'll just say THAT'S IT—I'VE HAD ENOUGH because that's how she's feeling. She needs to be assured you aren't going anywhere. The body might not be able to relax at this coming lesson. Please just let it be. Right now tension is also protection. s.s. [s.s. was "Small Sam"]

(I thought to myself: It wasn't enough getting advice from the piano. Now I'm getting advice from her inner kids!)

I sent Ariah a copy of the email, and she wrote back: "Damn. Well, at least I know I'm doing what I have to do—letting you know."

Ariah and I pressed forward, working with goals and objective ways to solve problems, rather than on their subjective underpinnings. Not surprisingly, she reported a parallel process with her own students. While Ariah was struggling to remain intact in the face of strong emotions, so too was a young student of hers. Ariah wrote about her autistic student, who constantly got upset whenever he made a mistake, running around saying negative things about himself.

Then one day, she reported, "His mother called me to tell me the following: He *initiated* his own practice session. He *identified* an error he had made. He *corrected* the error. Then he ran around saying, '*I'm a good piano player.*'"

Triumph: Ariah playing at a service in her synagogue. "There were over 300 people. . . . I was the first on the program and when I finished the room was SILENT. It was like getting a standing ovation."

Despair: Ariah back in the hospital for a manic episode, which mimicked a psychotic break. I spoke with her therapist, who called Ariah "extremely delicate, like a flower trying to blossom."

Blossoming was a challenge, as blood tests revealed conclusively that Ariah had lupus. She was angry at not having been taken seriously when she told them years before she thought she had lupus, and felt vindicated that she was right. Worse, there had been a shift in the medical view of her condition, or at least in Ariah's perception of that view. She told me her doctors no longer viewed her as an ongoing patient on an *acute* basis, but as a *chronic* patient. This demoralized her to the point where she said she felt like giving up. When she asked my advice, I hardly knew what to say, aware of the import of the prevailing medical view at the time. Somehow I managed to give her a possible alternative view, but I was grasping at straws myself.

"Try viewing this as a letting-go process," I advised. "Now that you and your doctors all seem to know and agree on what is going on with you, your system no longer has to struggle to make itself understood. Now your body can use its fighting energy for healing."

As part of her healing process, Ariah went through a burial ritual. On Mother's Day of our fifth year together, she dug a deep hole in her backyard and ceremonially buried items she had carefully crafted—symbols of the past she sought to lay to rest, such as the children she would never have. There were letters to important people in her life, and musings to bring closure in understanding her parents and realizing how much pain they themselves must have endured to have inflicted so much on her. She wrote to her alternate personalities, thanking them for giving up their autonomy "that we may together be whole."

In my studio, she went through burying motions by sitting on the floor with me as she symbolically put pieces of paper into a box, each with a label: "my unborn children, my alters Laura, Catherine, Small Sam," and so forth. She said Kaddish, the Jewish prayer for the dead, and solemnly covered the box with a shawl. Watching Ariah go through the ritual, I felt sorry that I wasn't able to sense the promise of renewal and healing that the ritual intended to represent.

However, the acts seemed to have given respite to Ariah, who reported that her relaxed body afforded her increased freedom of expression at the piano, and that she could play even while old demons taunted. And she could cry—with happiness. She taped words near her piano that I had often uttered when fear overtook her: "You are strong. You have overcome many obstacles in your life, and you will get past this one, too. Remember your love of music and let your piano support you in times of need."

Ending and the Tape

Without realizing that we were entering our last year together—our sixth—we began in earnest to exchange thoughts about our book. One day, Ariah brought in her account of our initial meeting:

> *My memory of actually meeting Margret is vague, but I do remember how I felt. Throughout my years of therapy I have often known what I needed to do to progress, and I have been fortunate enough to have therapists who have respected this aspect of my treatment. My battle with the piano, however, was different because I had never before had the chance to have the therapist and the piano with me at the same time. I needed someone who understood the physical and emotional strength it takes to be a musician. I also needed some-one who understood the spiritual and mental challenges of breaking free from the chains of post-traumatic stress disorder. Margret was not afraid of my pro-cess. She would trust me enough to allow me to experience my feelings in full so that I might integrate them into my present being. My therapy and musi-cal training with Margret has resulted in a level of psychological freedom at the piano, which I can only describe as being holy. "You intended to harm me, but God intended it for good to accomplish what is now being done . . ." (Gen. 50:20). Each time I play I cannot help but take a moment to praise God, thank Margret, and honor myself.*

We reviewed our years together, then previewed the future. We toasted the fact that Ariah's life had become richer—as musician, teacher and student of psychology. But we also discussed the chronic conditions that frequently crippled her ability to function. Of late she had had to rely on friends to drive her to her lessons, an hour and a half from home. Was it time for her to think of taking lessons nearer home with a piano teacher whose role would simply be to teach piano? At first with panic, then with perspective, Ariah saw that this was not only an ending but also a triumph on her part. It was a physical necessity, as well.

"This is very hard," she said. I concurred. She said, "I keep thinking, is Margret really trying to get rid of me? Is she punishing me? I can't imagine that you are, but, you know . . ."

"Yes, I knew that your old fears would crop up. And I don't think you actually believe them now." I looked at her with upturned brows.

"I think it's also hard to accept that this is for *me*," she exhaled. "That someone cares deeply enough to let me go, and not keep me in my cage. No one knows me like you do. But I think I can be frightened and still be okay. I'm going to *have* to be."

We set a date two months away to bring our work to a close.

One month later, she brought in a tape she had made specifically for me with a close friend she'd had for about fifteen years, since she was eighteen. The purpose of the tape, Ariah explained, was to lay to rest the ever-present question of whether the past she believed in was real or unconsciously created. This friend had borne witness to her fragmented life, traumatized states and alter personalities. Listening to the tape, it was easy to imagine two close friends sitting together in front of a tape recorder. While they discussed Ariah's history, they often broke out into peals of laughter, provoked by this friend's wry, *noir* humor. It was with great pleasure that I heard Ariah laughing so hard. Below, I quote at length from the tape to give readers its full flavor.

The Tape: History, Friendship, Laughter, Tears

Laughter began when her friend Wanda related meeting Ariah's alter Elizabeth. As alters emerged, Wanda searched for the appropriate means with which to address them:

> *Wanda: I met Elizabeth when she was 18. When 'she and company' were 18—[pause] . . . when your physical body was 18. [Laughter] Elizabeth was creating non-profit organizations and writing a song and being on TV and you were taking piano lessons with P. It was a huge part of your life. The basic facts of Elizabeth were piano and abuse. She studied singing, acting, drama, psychology and later religion. She was outgoing, dynamic, ambitious—a real control freak and very focused. You already had two incidences of losing time, although you didn't know that was what it was called. One was when you told me you woke up in the kitchen in the dark with no clothes on and a big knife in your hand, and I said, 'WHOA. . . .' It was the most helpful response I could think of at the time.*

I couldn't help but join their giggling. Wanda went on with Ariah's history as I listened intently to the tape:

W: *One day you called and said, 'I don't remember you but my therapist says you're really important to me so could you come and visit me?' 'Who are you?' I asked. You said, 'I'm Samantha.' What had transpired was the last two years had been erased from your mind. You thought you were 17 and in a hospital because your mother had beaten you so badly . . . you guys had been going to a wedding and were in a parking lot and you got into an argument and she started hitting you. . . .*

Ariah: [Loudly] *Yes! That happened.*

W: *I know. That was the last thing you—as Samantha—remembered. So at that point I'm guessing you switched to Elizabeth, stayed Elizabeth for two years until you got yourself out of the house, into school, got some help . . . until Elizabeth could no longer hold it together anymore. You started having those weird blackout periods, lost time—that's when you thought you were in the hospital.*

A: [Interrupting] *That must have been very weird for you.*

W: *What was weirder was trying to tell you what you'd done and still stay trustworthy in your eyes. It's a lot of responsibility to have somebody's history in your hands and try and tell it back in a way that doesn't distort their perceptions in any way. Yeah, it was weird. . . . When you were Samantha, you were so much more emotional, more spontaneous than Elizabeth. And you had child alters . . . and you were in art therapy. You were in the hospital for two months then, and I visited you twice a week. Elizabeth didn't come out until you were out of the hospital and living on your own. It was hard for Elizabeth to come out because they really preferred Samantha at the hospital.*

A: *I think if there was one mistake in my treatment, that was it—I don't think they should ever favor one alter over the others—they're all part of the same person. . . .*

W: *Especially because Elizabeth was the one who got you to safety, and out of your parents' house. She found a lawyer, got mental health. Elizabeth was a survivor. If Samantha could have done it, she would have—but she checked out in the parking lot, leaving you in Elizabeth's capable hands. Then you came out . . . and we went to Disneyland—the trip from hell.*

There was uproarious laughter as Wanda proceeded to describe that trip and the challenges she faced with Ariah and "the people on your beat," as she called Ariah's other personalities:

W: *That was the first time I dealt with your alters, and I wasn't sure what was politically correct or who you were . . . and you didn't always know, yourself. . . . So here we are driving to Disneyland, and all of a sudden you weren't you.*

A: *How did you know?*

W: *Your tone of voice changed.* [Here Wanda switched to a high-pitched imitation of Ariah's voice.] *Where are we?* [Back to her normal voice.] *So I'm obviously talking to a kid, but I didn't know if I could say, 'Who are you? How old are you?'*

As Wanda related the dialogue, she went back and forth between her voice and the child's:

W: [In the child's voice] *Four.* [In Wanda's normal voice] *Can you read?*

Child: *No.*

W: *Do you have anyone in there who can read?*

At this point I started laughing.

Child: No.

W: Hey, could you go get someone there who can read? Go! Scoot! Scram! I need someone to help navigate.

A: [Interjecting] Little did you know, none of me could help navigate. [More laughter. Then, more seriously:]

A: Remember Valerie?

W: I never actually met Valerie. On that trip you knew about Sam, Small Sam, Elizabeth, Kylie, and other people who lived in your beat. . . . That whole weekend I didn't know how to handle it. We'd be at Disneyland and you'd go, 'I want a hotdog!' We'd go over to the hotdog stand, and then you'd go, 'I hate hotdogs.' Boy, did that frustrate me! I remember saying, 'Okay. Somebody wanted a hotdog so somebody better get out here and eat a hotdog.' And you had a headache the whole time. I think you were really over stimulated.

A: Yes. And I was afraid of everything. . . . Snow White, Cinderella. . . .

W: Everything scared you. The moon, stars. Everything was loaded with symbolism. I had no idea Snow White was so fraught with terror.

In between descriptions of having to cope with spontaneous appearances of people on Ariah's "beat," Wanda related Ariah's ongoing hospitalizations, living in a halfway house, struggling to make sense out of her fragmented life:

W: You said Valerie ought to be streetwalking. As Valerie, you didn't know that stuff wasn't happening right then—the beatings and rape. I had to reassure you that everything was okay. I remember I gave you an aspirin for your imaginary soreness from having been beaten. You took a bath . . . and then you came out and said, 'I sure like my feet!'

And they giggled together.

> W: *'Who are you?' I said. It was one of the kids. We had a nice conversa-*
> *tion about your feet, and then in a blink of an eye, you changed—to Valerie?*
> *I hoped I was guessing right. I think you were afraid I was going to leave you*
> *alone. You were losing a lot of time then. The doctor at the hospital said you*
> *were one of the true multiples he'd met. Then you went to Sacramento. That*
> *was the worst time—when all the alters came out. You were suicidal. You were*
> *really fragmented all the time. I mean some of it was funny—like when Small*
> *Sam called and said, 'Have you seen Sam or Elizabeth anywhere? How about*
> *Mollie or Celeste? What about Rebecca? I haven't seen them in three days.' And*
> *I said: 'Honey, if you haven't seen them, I sure as hell haven't either.' Hard time.*
> *You were trying to go to school. You took your backpack and books . . . and your*
> *coloring book and crayons . . . because if you switched in the middle of class,*
> *your kids would have something to do.*

They giggled again.

Ariah was taking classes at a state college. Wanda continued describing those days:

> W: *You were switching several times a day and starting to define your*
> *alters by figuring out what roles they had. That was when you made the chart—*
> *to show which ones were your cores—and you figured what their jobs were. You*
> *had three main alters . . . and all the others split off from them. After you made*
> *the chart, you stepped back and said, 'Hey, you forgot me.' That was Liz—her*
> *first time out. Her job was to be neurotic about [unintelligible word]—and*
> *some of the kids' jobs were to see that you ate healthy foods. You were calling in*
> *the middle of the night, scared of demons. . . . You were not certain what was*
> *today, and what was a long time ago. . . .*

> A: *Yeah, that was what was happening. And Rebecca and Celeste, later*

integrated into one alter.

W: *As you started getting more co-conscious [aware of her alters], you realized that one of your alters was your higher, angelic, inner self-helper. You said then she was an angel. You were very religious at the time. It was her name, Ariah, that you consciously chose to identify with when your core personality became dominant. You figured if you were going to revert to one of your alters, you'd revert to her. It was Ariah who asked me to stay with you for two weeks. And I said, 'Look, angel person, I have a job.'*

A: *It's a good thing I chose Ariah, because if I'd chosen Mollie and reverted, I'd be seven years old all the time. Mollie and a lot of other alters never wanted to grow up—they got stuck at a young age. Then there was Harriet, who came as a baby inside my feet. . . .*

W: *Right. When you got all excited, your feet would move and that would be Harriet. But she ended up older and wiser—she grew. I have letters, like the one Harriet wrote when she was going to integrate.*

Wanda then revealed what it felt like as she witnessed the integration of Ariah's alters:

W: *I was pissed when Harriet integrated without talking to me first. It was weird because as you started to integrate, you could see pieces of your alters but the characteristics were not as strong. I missed parts that were distinctive to them. It was almost more disjointed for me to be talking to just one person all the time. But also, it was a little easier because when you called and identified yourself as 'Me,' I didn't have to say, 'Okay, well you have forty people in there named Me. Could you be more specific? To which Me do I have the pleasure of speaking?'*

Ariah gave me permission to make a transcript of the tape so I could read and reread it at leisure. Wanda's devotion and friendship, and the two friends' ability to laugh at the tragic aspects of Ariah's life, gave me additional insight into the poignant human dimension of Ariah's strength, talents and challenges. This intimate glimpse into the myriad threads of a dissociated personality like hers, so far removed from most people's experience, so far removed from my own, was revelatory.

The Cycles of Life

During our last month together, Ariah prepared to leave her cage and exercise her wings. I helped her find a teacher near her home who had studied with a student of mine, and who would give Ariah space to be herself, in addition to guiding her musically.

"I want to discuss how much progress I've made to be able to see a piano teacher who isn't a therapist," she told me.

"You start," I said.

Ariah then listed many occasions when she had played without fear, occasions when she had not collapsed in despair at disappointments or heard punishing demon voices, and when she had not "split" after being overwhelmed with emotion.

"What about your teaching?" I prodded.

Ariah smiled and told me the story of one of her high school students, whose musical evolution closely mirrored Ariah's. Cindy, a senior, wrote an essay for her AP English class on "A Moment of Significance" in her life. The essay detailed her early desire for piano lessons and the early recognition of her talent. As a teenager, however, she lost interest and stopped lessons.

"I vowed," Cindy wrote, "never to sit at a piano again." But the longing returned. When it did, Cindy found Ariah, who prepared her for a performance at her school. Cindy wrote in her essay:

> This time it was my decision. I was doing it because "I" wanted to, not because "they" wanted me to. I found a teacher who let me be myself through my music and who taught me to love my piano; to appreciate every movement my hands made and every note of music that filled the air. For the first time in all my years of playing, the piano became my home, my place of comfort. . . . As I heard my name called and walked to the beautiful grand piano I knew there was no place I would rather be. I was going home.

"I love that story," I burst out. "You helped Cindy back to her love of playing. What care and sensitivity you showed her! Hopefully, you will continue showing the same care and sensitivity to yourself."

While in this jovial mood, Ariah remembered a dream she'd had recently. "I'm in a psychiatric hospital and overhear a nurse telling abused children, 'Let go, let God.' I go over to the nurse and say, 'That won't work. These children can't hear words like that in their present condition.'" Ariah looked pensive. "Those children are me. I know them."

The hardest part of stopping our work together for Ariah was the fact that I was the only person to whom she'd confided certain parts of her history, and who deeply understood the importance of music to her and the enormity of her struggle to reclaim it. She wrote in her diary:

> It was important that someone understand the magnitude of emotional and cognitive material music brought up for me, and honor my artistic as well as psychological process. I could not have done this in a therapist's office because it was being with the piano that brought the flashbacks.

In turn, I told Ariah I felt privileged to have earned her trust and witnessed her work. It had been a stunning experience sitting with her pain, which I often had to sit with long after she'd left our sessions. She knew that I viewed her as more than a PTSD victim and larger than the sum of her diagnoses. She knew that I saw her as a woman struggling to reconnect with the wellspring of her vitality, with music the inroad to that vitality. I did not express the reservations I felt about whether there would be a rosy future or happiness ahead, but I hoped she would never give up the struggle.

When Ariah came in for her last session, she brought a cassette tape and placed it in my tape recorder. We faced each other, separated by the heaviness of our emotions. A bittersweet moment. It reminded me of the times I took each of my sons to college, moments overflowing with joy, hope and promise, simultaneously felt with the heavy heart of a mother watching her children take flight.

Pointing to the tape recorder, Ariah wanted me to record how I viewed her.

Speaking into the tape recorder, I said: "I saw a woman who never gave up, never gave up. Who kept moving, through teachers when necessary, and through therapists and doctors. I saw a woman who set up a music studio. I watched what you did to come here. All those hurdles—staying in hotels when driving home was painful; getting a driver when driving was impossible; having lessons on the phone when you couldn't come at all. And another thing . . . " I smiled. "You know how to use the medical system: how to get the right kind of medical, emotional support—that's brilliant."

"Yes, I know how to try to get what I need. I'm proud of that, too." The compelling voice of the woman sitting across from me had gravitas, substance.

"I have to share something with you." Ariah said softly. "I saw my rabbi, a woman, who I've told about the sexual abuse and how sad I am that I'll never have children. We went to the building where the Mikvah [ritual cleansing] is in [Ariah's hometown] and the rabbi had a prayer book. We said Kaddish [a prayer for the dead] for the people in my family who are dead to me, a separate prayer for the children I will never have. Then I went to the bathing area, and she stood behind the closed door. As I bathed, we gave thanks for my survival."

Ariah saw me looking at her intently and asked what I was thinking.

"I'm thinking about the cycle of life, and how the Mikvah beautifully begins your next cycle, much as it had when you went there the night before our first session."

That first cleansing heralded the period in Ariah's life when her musical and traumatized selves were to unite. Now, once again, immersed in the cleansing waters of renewal, Ariah was readying herself to move on.

Postscript

Shortly after our last session, Ariah sent me the following note:

> I am comforted in the knowledge that even if I fade away, someone—you—has witnessed the melodies of my soul, those that sang, raged, feared, hoped, trusted, transformed, and loved. Thank you.

METAPHORS: LINKS BETWEEN MUSIC AND PSYCHE

These case studies, in which musicians seek wholeness through music, illustrate how interwoven that search is with the search for knowing oneself. Daniel Barenboim declares that "music teaches us that everything is connected."[30] People brave enough to follow where those connections lead—like those in this book—ultimately find their way to self-discovery with its attendant poetry and pain. Poetry there is, when we glimpse the possibility of realizing our fullest self, the person we were born to become. Pain there is, when we discover that who we have become does not reflect our true self. Discerning the metaphors embedded in music and their relevance to our personal lives helps bridge the gap between our false and our true selves. The more we uncover the lessons of those metaphors, the more fully we inhabit our humanity and place in the world. Soul-work, whether at couch or at piano, is about making connections that uncover our true self.

When Sound Becomes Existence

In music, connections begin even before the first note. "Don't just start to play," I implore my students. "Come out of the silence." But students rush to begin playing because silence is scary. Alexander once said, "I have a horror of calm. Rests are very hard for me." And another student declared, "I have a fear of open spaces—I get lost in spaces, and disoriented," when I pointed out that she'd ignored a rest in the middle of a bar.

What is the fear of silence or resting? Perhaps it is that when the connections normally made through activity or sound are interrupted, we are left feeling unmoored. Maybe it harkens back to our prehistoric selves when sudden silence might have signaled danger and it was incumbent on survival to heighten the senses in order to locate its source. Before playing or before an open space in music, when there are no wild animals around, where then put our focus? Without an object, we are left anxious and race through the silence to ground ourselves with sound.

Connecting to silence around music is analogous to being in touch with the silence inside us. Every silence has its own dynamic energy, no matter how still,

residing as it does within its particular context. The silence of a predatory crea-
ture in the jungle differs vastly from that of bucolic sheep grazing in the field.
The silence before the attention-grabbing C-Minor chord that opens Beethoven's
Pathétique Sonata contrasts sharply with that before the gentler, taking-us-by-the-
hand A-flat-major chord that opens his Op. 110 Sonata. To play a piece, therefore,
one starts by connecting to the silence out of which the music emerges. Doing so
involves focusing on and animating that silence, which, at its best, takes us out of
feeling self-conscious and anxious.

For Alexander, beautiful sound—which is what we normally strive for in playing—took on a life of its own. Among other things, it was the symbol of his acceptance: If he produced the perfect sound—the interface between himself and the
outside world—he would be seen as perfect, too. But that quest hindered his ability to move forward and develop the other elements that contribute to fine musi-
cianship. It also hindered him from entering his full personality as a musician and
as a gay man. I think of the child in an unhappy environment who, in her anxiety
to please, suffers unending turmoil attempting to find the right combination of
words and actions to attain her parents' love. Since sound is more primitive than
words in early development, the search to *sound* perfect speaks to an early hunger
for acceptance.

While sound partially served as a metaphor for acceptance with Alexander, it
often says something even more powerful: the statement that "I exist." When such
a meaning attaches to sound, untenable internal conflict can result.

For musicians for whom music was a means of hiding from an otherwise intol-
erable environment, their connection to music becomes a refuge, a place to speak
their truth while hiding. Playing for others then risks being exposed and possibly
punished. At the same time, being seen and heard for who we are is a basic human
need. In ideal situations, parents supply such acceptance through the mirroring
they provide for their babies. But in a dangerous environment, one is caught in the
psychic dilemma of "hear me, see me/don't hear me, don't see me." This can be
crazy-making. Such a vortex of contradictory needs has the power to bring a person
to the brink of feeling annihilated. Feelings get translated into symbols of black-
ness and ice, sometimes accompanied by the fragmenting of one's core personality into dissociated parts. Behaviors that cause trauma are not limited to severe

emotional or physical abuse. The level of deprivation someone experiences in his natural development may be objectively mild, yet still cause havoc with the normal maturation process.

In such cases, the tasks of being seen, being heard and feeling safe become challenging. With Celeste, the fear that followed making her first big sound with ease was clearly registered in her face: an almost invisible retraction of muscles, an immediate sitting back and away from the keyboard, eyes glaring. Suddenly, after hiding so long behind the invisibility of her tiny sound, the first big sound she produced on the piano announced her own presence—and it frightened her. As you have already read, it took much couch-work to incorporate this promise of a larger Celeste into the fabric of her personality.

When Ease Becomes Effort

Playing with technical and physical ease would seem to be a desirable goal. Yet striving to achieve ease is thwarted by the powerful metaphor in our anxiety-driven era that links hard work to self-image, importance and worth. As one student quipped after I showed him an easy way to play a passage: "It scares me when things are as simple as this."

Celeste, whose big sound frightened her, likened her compulsion to work hard at the keyboard to her compulsive housecleaning. Is this not, in fact, the metaphor for our society's worshipping at the altar of "the work ethic," that long-established moral imperative dividing the virtuous from the nonvirtuous?

I ask: What would happen if you stopped tackling the piano as if you were cleaning house? What feelings lie concealed beneath this drive to activity? The answers: "I'd feel like a sloth." "I hear my mother/my father/my teacher/my priest scolding me for laziness." "I'd feel sad/angry/happy." "I'd see my neighbor looking askance at what a comfy life I have."

"And your neighbor," I ask teasingly, "does your neighbor scrub as hard?"

"Oh no, she has a cleaning lady." That actually *was* Celeste's response!

The concept that achievement is possible by working efficiently and without tension often necessitates changing mental patterns as well as muscle patterns. Because everything is connected, I often suggest that a student make some small change in her nonmusical life before making a change at the keyboard. It was easier for Celeste, you may recall, to change the seating at dinner than to become more present at the keyboard. Once a small step is taken, it can lead to larger steps until there is a paradigm shift in the implied metaphor. For Celeste, that shift would be from "I myself am not worthy; I'm here to help others" to "I myself am worthy; I don't have to leap up to help others."

"It would take an act of faith," one student responded to my suggestion of releasing tension in her hand, especially in the fifth finger poised in the air, teacup style. "Just the idea that the keyboard is there and will support my fingers takes an enormous amount of trust. Will it support me when I need it to?"

And finally, as the experience of ease becomes—well, let's say—easier, the sense of wonder translates into tears and a feeling that, as one student said, "I'm not doing anything. It's just . . . just about being present."

I nodded, yes. "You're saying you don't have to work hard to be yourself."

When Ease Becomes Betrayal

While playing with ease might feel like a betrayal of society's caveat to work hard, it can also conjure up the feeling of other kinds of betrayal: of the past, of those who have died, of parents who worked hard all their lives. Remember Alexander, whose parents had been immigrants working day and night in their new country to provide for their family? What right do such children have to find themselves through music without working as hard? What right to take time to "Sit-in-the-Release," to breathe, be still, listen and pay attention to their bodies and their music? What right did my student, a young widow, have to play her beloved *Goldberg Variations,* by Bach, without tension when her joyful, young husband had died prematurely? We would need to reframe her music as a testament to his joie de vivre rather than as a betrayal.

"That's exactly what he would have wanted," she said, smiling and tearful.

Rhythm as a Life Force

Rhythm is a fundamental, life-giving source, keeping body and soul together. Our survival depends on the regular rhythm of our breathing and heartbeat. When the doctor discovers an irregular heartbeat, she more than likely prescribes medication. Our heartbeat—our internal rhythm—not only keeps us alive but also is intimately connected to our physical and emotional states.

Walking is an example of how our internal rhythm is conveyed physically. Maintaining regular rhythm in walking involves fluidity and the slight lifting of the body upward with each step taken forward. Maintaining this regularity in moving forward conveys confidence. For Celeste, we have seen that playing unsteadily served to hold her feelings—especially anger—in check so they wouldn't overwhelm her. With so much psychic energy invested in restraining herself, there was little left for moving forward.

The duality that inheres in the concept of rhythm is freedom and containment, and music reminds us that this balance is requisite for a sense of well-being. Think of the child's impulse to explore only when safe in the parent's presence, or of the disorientation in the child who has no limits set on behavior. Music teachers often have to lead students, *in loco parentis,* from random wanderings of tempo. Students may balk, but in the end they feel relief at having been safely reined in.

Unsteadiness of rhythm often harbors inner unsteadiness. One middle-aged gay man I taught expressed the fear of not being "right enough just being who I am," and his fear was reflected in his irregular rhythm. "It goes back to my sexuality and passion. I mean, I come from Southern gentility, goddammit. Everything was just swept under the rug."

To live at either end of the rhythmic extremes—unrestrained freedom or rigidity—is isolating. It prevents fluidity of feelings, of perspective, of action. And it prevents making those vital connections to the hearts of other people, and to the soul of music. It takes courage to realize that music is more than the written notes. But it takes discipline not to intrude on the musical meaning. It is then that true expression can flow. Such give-and-take is comparable to the give-and-take between two people in conversation, when each carefully listens to the other and responds accordingly.

When Fast Becomes Fear

Playing with speed is another musical challenge that can conjure up anxiety. "I'm afraid of playing fast, afraid I'll float into the air," one student told me. Fear of floating away was also the reason she played everything *legato*—connecting notes to each other—with fingers that never left the safety of the keys. It kept her from playing with different kinds of touches—short, long and somewhere in-between. A heavy foot on the sustaining pedal (which keeps the notes sounding) was another way to prevent floating away.

This student started studying with me as an adult returning to the piano after years without lessons. With her natural gifts, she had mastered much of the technique I taught her, but there was a breakdown at playing with speed.

"There's this knot in my chest when I start playing fast. It's just a lot of anxiety." Breathing directly to her knot did not help. I searched for something to do, as she looked at me expectantly. I had her put her hands in the center of the piano, resting on keys without playing, while Sitting-in-the-Release. She was able to calm herself in that position. I had her quickly fling her arms from the center of the keyboard to the highest keys and back again without playing. Then from center a quick fling down to the lowest notes and back. She kept flinging her hands first high then low as fast as she could without playing a note until that felt easy. But she balked at the thought of extending the exercise into playing an actual scale with any speed.

"I'm afraid I'll play wrong notes."

"And then?" I asked. We had circled this issue before, and I sounded like a broken record to myself. But the answer was new.

"Well, maybe I'm afraid I'll fail my father's high expectations." Her face suddenly brightened as she made that association.

"Is that only with music or in other areas of your life, as well?" She raised her eyebrows at my question, tilted her head and looked out the window as if searching for the answer outside.

"That's interesting. It's only here. At work when I make a mistake, I say, 'Oh nuts!' and move on."

Then, breaking the cardinal rule of not visualizing what you *don't* want, I asked her to imagine playing very fast, making a mistake, immediately saying, "Oh nuts," and continuing to play. She closed her eyes. In a few moments she opened them with an "aha!" expression on her face—eyes wide, smiling. I looked at her with anticipation at what she would say.

"I got it! Anxiety is only a mental construct that I myself place on that 'knot' feeling. It isn't anxiety unless I call it that. I could call it anything I want," she wisely concluded. It didn't immediately result in playing at the lightning speed of pianist Martha Argerich, but it did open up the possibility that speed was learnable. At her father's eighty-seventh birthday celebration, her gift was a performance of three Rachmaninoff Preludes, only two of which were slow.

Dread at the End of a Phrase

John, an engineer, had recently switched to my studio after studying with another teacher for many years, but he remained friends with students from that studio. When he played Mozart's *Sonata in D Major, K. 576* for me, he raced through the ending of one phrase and into the next, ignoring rests, ignoring beats.

What happens at those points in a piece where one musical thought ends and another begins? It turns out, a lot. One idea ends and another begins, like one person leaving a party as another enters. The gracious host bids an unhurried good-bye to the first while happily welcoming the newcomer.

John quietly mulled over the question of what happened for him at those musical transitions. I sensed him struggling over divulging his thoughts. We didn't know each other well yet as student and teacher. Finally he said, "I'm still working on my transition to your studio," and he mentioned missing both the teacher and the students he left behind. I smiled, thinking with admiration how quickly he associated the musical end of a *phrase* with the real-life end of a *phase*. Acknowledging the loss he felt, we discussed ways to make the transition easier. He devised the plan of continuing to perform with his former teacher's students at their homes, but not at the teacher's studio. He agreed he would join the student gatherings I hold in my studio.

The issue of transitioning between musical segments had been addressed but not yet solved. John surprised me once again with his response after I pointed out that he doubled the tempo at bar 41 of the Mozart Sonata, a bar that bridged a rhythmic section with a melodic one.

"It's like the end of the world," he said, smiling but not joking. "Like Christ coming down to earth with the first notes of this bar, and then ascending to heaven." John looked like he had even surprised himself by saying that. "I don't like endings. It's like Mummy's gone and they're destroying your teddy bear. I want to get through this as quickly as possible."

Who knew a single bar could contain so much hidden meaning?!

Metaphors conjured up by music are powerful. Their meaning derives from personal experience as well as universal constructs. In Daniel Barenboim's eloquent book *Music Quickens Time*, we read about the relation between the elements of music and the universal emotions ascribed to them. Quoting Aristotle, Barenboim writes that rhythm supplies imitations of anger and courage, and melody of gentleness and temperance.[31]

It makes sense, then, that this particular Mozart bar challenged John, for its implicit meanings welled up from both personal and universal sources. There was a suggested forcefulness in the initial repeated notes of the bar. And there were John's personal feelings associated with endings and loss. One short rest bridges the two sensibilities. By living in the connection of that moment—as force gives way to gentleness—the meaning nestled in that short, musical moment becomes organic and dynamic.

Paying attention to music's moments is paying attention to our psyche. Conversely, paying attention to ourselves is uncovering our personal music. It signifies inhabiting our own lives. The all-too-human quest for wholeness may prove elusive. Yet, in the process of searching, we become richer and fuller with each connection the psyche makes to the ineffable world within, to the ineffable world beyond.

SECTION IV

TERMS & EXERCISES

xcept for the exercise Sitting-in-the-Release, all exercises in this book are taken from my book *Passionate Practice: The Musician's Guide to Learning, Memorizing and Performing* (Oakland, CA: Regent Press, 2002). They provide the means to calm oneself mentally and physically, and to remain alert and grounded in the present. They all require patience and practice.

The Automatic Relax Response and The Calming Light

These are basic calming exercises. They focus awareness on your natural breathing as it moves downward into your abdomen, grounding your energy and allowing calmness to permeate your body.

The Automatic Relax Response: Sit in a comfortable chair, arms in lap, feet touching the floor. Keep your mouth slightly open to ensure that you don't clench your jaw. Focus your awareness on your natural breathing, and ride your breath as it gently passes through your open mouth, downward through your chest and into your abdomen. Feel your waist expanding and contracting with your breathing. It is important to remain aware of the *downward* motion of your breathing, for that is what grounds your energy and serves as an antidote to the distracting thoughts occurring *up* in your head.

The Calming Light: Picture a point of light (or another calming image) at the spot where your breath ends. With practice, this image becomes your *cue*, directly leading you to—that is, *cueing*—calmness. You can use this cue at any time, not only to deflect anxiety, but also to ground yourself and to return your attention to the present moment when your focus wanders. Being both *relaxed and alert*—in short, *R/A*—allows you to deal calmly with any situation at hand.

Puppy-Dog Hands and Magic Carpet

Puppy-Dog Hand is what I call the hand's default position: the feeling in the fingers when they aren't being used—such as when you're resting, or when you're walking with arms freely swaying. And Magic Carpet, in my practice, is an invisible force that raises and lowers the arms from beneath, so they feel as if they are floating up to the instrument (or desk, or other surface), saving you from having to exert energy to move.

The following exercises help you explore these concepts.

Puppy-Dog Hands: Take a walk and sway your arms freely! Pay attention to how your hands feel while swinging freely. Then sit at your instrument, swing your arms into place as if ready to play and keep your fingers free of tension. Avoiding unnecessary tension in the hands helps prevent the cycle of *physical tension producing anxiety producing negative thoughts producing more tension.*

Magic Carpet: Sit at your instrument and cue yourself to *R/A* (see above) with arms resting in your lap, fingers released in their relaxed Puppy-Dog position. As you continue to breathe, let your arms become heavy. Then let your Magic Carpet glide under your arms and bring them up to your instrument—while retaining their heaviness. Practice allowing your arms to be raised and lowered by the Magic Carpet while keeping your hands in the Puppy-Dog position. It is especially important when the music demands big leaps between hand positions at the keyboard to feel your arms *being transported*—because it is at those split seconds that anxiety creeps in.

Strengthening the Sensory System

This exercise is designed to strengthen sensory awareness—particularly the audio, visual and kinesthetic channels. (In *Passionate Practice,* I further break down the sensory system into eight distinct channels.) Strengthening sensory awareness grounds the performer by producing an internal loop among the senses, thereby minimizing the space in which anxiety can lodge.

Successful practice engages *all* the senses in focusing on how the music sounds, how the hands look and how the body and hands feel. No matter what the emotional intensity of the music, hands and body should reflect ease in producing the music. In a word: Good practice sounds good, feels comfortable in hands and arms, and looks good (that is, not tense).

Strengthening the Sensory System: Take a walk anywhere that's safe— inside or outside. Experience the environment around you through a single sense, and see how much you can learn from that sense alone. If plausible, use earplugs or eye patches to help block out individual senses. After you've gotten the hang of it, experience the environment through two, then three of the senses. Notice how those changes affect your relation to the environment, your focus and your concentration. Later, when you are at your instrument, play a note or chord and experience that sound through each of your individual senses. *Listen* with huge ears glued to the sound. *Look* at the position of your hands. Then, be aware of how your hands *feel* in that position, and how the internal kinesthetic of your body accompanying that moment *feels* as well.

Sitting-in-the-Release

This simple yet powerful exercise integrates the others into one concept. It calms you while aligning your breathing, your senses and your focus.

Sitting-in-the-Release: Cue yourself to a state of calm, using the image you have chosen in the Calming Light exercise (above), and continue breathing as you feel the weight from your shoulders released into your arms. When your body is relaxed and your mind alert—that is, when you are in the R/A stance—continue breathing as you connect with the surrounding environment through your senses: *hearing* sounds or silence, *seeing* details, *feeling* your responses. Without hurrying, sit a few moments in this position of release: breathing, using your senses and sitting in the calm.

This all-encompassing technique, which can be done anywhere, grounds and contains your energy and attention. In *Passionate Practice*, I detail how to use it in both the learning process and the relearning process, when old patterns need to be altered. Do give yourself plenty of time to learn it.

Walking: Action with Simultaneous Release

For most of us, walking is a natural, comfortable and unconscious act. Each leg moves effortlessly with an invisible force. There is no tension in calf or thigh, and toes don't clutch the ground. Once a foot is down in front, weight seamlessly shifts to that leg, and you take a step forward. And more importantly, you find that your step includes a bounce, not a thud, and your body experiences an upward thrust, ready to move forward again. It is as if the ground under your foot meets you partway and cushions that foot from hitting too hard.

Your body naturally activates your muscles and joints, not to mention your brain, in this process. But you do not consciously need to add activity to effect the movement. You simply *will* it, and the body does the rest. At the same time, if your arms are free from, say, holding groceries, they are likely to swing freely without holding tension.

While our bodies were created for walking, and not explicitly for playing Beethoven, we can apply this same primal pattern of action with simultaneous release to help instill ease in our artistry. Here's how.

Walking with Simultaneous Release: First take a few turns around the room, noticing how your feet propel you forward; allow your arms to swing as you walk. Notice that you do not need to clutch or tighten leg muscles or toes; and notice how your weight transfers from back leg to front. Finally, notice how your body springs upward with each step.

Now at your instrument, let your hands be lifted by your Magic Carpet (notice the passive voice) to the keyboard with the same feeling they had when freely swinging as you walked. As the hands descend, the full weight of the arms—like that of the legs—is released into the desired keys. When the hands move, whether to a note close by or far away, they move like the legs, transported in space without tension.

This concept of movement—*action with simultaneous release*—is a universal concept in martial arts, sports and music-making.

Body Stances

If, as I suggest, the body is a brain that moves, we are happily provided with two dynamic resources in our search for fullness: the cognitive-analytic-brain, and the physical-body-brain. Separately, each holds the vital information we need to create the story of our life and to meet its challenges. Together, they form a synergistic force of such magnitude that changes necessary for healing and growth can be realized.

Because the body is often more informative than the mind in uncovering the answers we seek, we need to let our bodies teach us about ourselves. We should inhabit, respect and communicate with our bodies in as many ways as we can devise, just as we continually exercise our brains. Here are some suggestions for doing that.

The Three-Pose Exercise When Facing Challenges: Earlier in this book I described the Three-Pose Exercise, which I created to take the prickles out of a challenging event. The first pose represents the actual event. While imagining that event, let's say I find myself stooping over, my arms stiffly embracing my body and my brows furrowed. Then I let my body segue into a stance—the second pose—that represents my life up to that point. I may find myself with my left foot stepping back, and my arms reaching left. From there, I let my body take me to the third pose, representing all the moments after the event, and find myself standing upright and looking ahead with outstretched arms.

Then I put the three stances together in a seamless, fluid movement. The stances are no longer discrete moments: They become part of a dance. Working physically alleviates my anxiety, allowing my brain to pursue the hard work of meeting the challenge that provoked the anxiety in the first place.

The Playing-Around Exercise to Bring Light to a Problem: Think of something occupying your thoughts. It could be a musical phrase or an entire piece. It could be an issue you want to solve, or an undesirable feeling. Without judging or censoring yourself, let your body assume a position—that is, a pose or a stance that represents that event. Let yourself actually *become* that stance, give it a voice and let it speak. You might then dialogue with it, and finally give it movement. See where it takes you and let yourself be surprised. You may find allies where you least expect.

Your Own Creative Exercises: Be creative in making up exercises that tap into your body's wisdom and that pull your mind and your body into alliance.

NOTES

1. Daniel Barenboim. *Music Quickens Time*. London: Verso, 2008, p. 108.
2. George Eliot. *The Lifted Veil: Brother Jacob*. (1859.) Oxford: Oxford University Press, 1999, p. 4.
3. Diane Ackerman. *A Natural History of the Senses*. New York: Vintage, 1990, p. 210.
4. Joshua Halberstam. *A Seat at the Table: A Novel of Forbidden Choices*. Naperville, IL: Sourcebooks Landmark, 2009, p. 38.
5. Katie Hafner. *A Romance on Three Legs: Glenn Gould's Obsessive Quest for the Perfect Piano*. New York: Bloomsbury, 2008, p. 11.
6. Daniel Barenboim. *Music Quickens Time*. New York: Verso, 2008, p. 108.
7. Jan Swafford. *Johannes Brahms: A Biography*. New York: Knopf, 1997, p. 42.
8. Daniel James Brown. *The Boys in the Boat: Nine Americans and Their Epic Quest for Gold at the 1936 Berlin Olympics*. Large print edition. New York, San Francisco, Farmington Hills, MI: Gale / Cengage Learning, 2014, p. 303.
9. Brendan Gill. *Here at the New Yorker*. New York: Random House, 1975, p. 163.
10. David Benioff. *City of Thieves*. Plume / Penguin: New York, 2009, p. 165
11. Susan S. Phillips. *Candlelight*. New York: Morehouse Publishing, 2008, p. 14.
12. Daniel J. Levitin. *This Is Your Brain on Music: The Science of a Human Obsession*. New York: Penguin, 2006, p. 57.
13. Richard Leppert. *The Sight of Sound: Music, Representation, and the History of the Body*. Berkeley: University of California Press, 1993, p. xx.
14. Ibid., p. 87.
15. Malia Wollan. "How to Ride a Bull." *New York Times Magazine*. May 31, 2015, p. 23.
16. Stéphane Mallarmé's letter to Eugène Lefébure, May 17, 1867, in Bradford

Cook, *Mallarmé*, p. 95 (quoted in Stanley Burnshaw, *The Seamless Web*, New York: Braziller, 1970, p. 301).

17. Claudio Arrau, interviewed in "The Art of the Piano," KQED Radio, 1999.

18. Music Teachers' Association of California, State Conference, 2011.

19. Video. *Richter: The Enigma.*

20. Charles Rosen. *Piano Notes: The World of the Pianist.* New York: Free Press, 2002, p. 27.

21. Susan S. Phillips, PhD. "Sabbath Living." *Radix Magazine*: 2006, p. 32.

22. Stanley Burnshaw. *The Seamless Web.* New York: Braziller, 1970, p. 91.

23. Egon Petri and Alexander Libermann. Lectures on "The Art and Technique of Pianoforte Playing," compiled over ten years at Mills College, by Robert Sheldon, Associate Professor of Piano, University of Missouri.

24. Ibid.

25. Ibid.

26. William Fifield. *In Search of Genius.* New York: William Morrow and Company, 1982, p. 107.

27. Haruki Murakami. *Kafka on the Shore.* New York: Vintage, 2005, p. 225.

28. See *Children of the Holocaust*, by Helen Epstein.

29. See Dr. Rachel Yehuda's work in epigenetics, including the concept that environment can change DNA.

30. Barenboim. *Music Quickens Time.* p. 108.

31. Ibid., p. 6.

ACKNOWLEDGMENTS

Many are the people whose support and enthusiasm have seen me through the writing of this book. My writing partner, Dr. Susan Phillips, has been stalwart in her encouragement and patience. Her insightful readings were accomplished with her usual aplomb, good nature and love. In addition, her own commitment to writing served as inspiration for me during those times when I questioned my own.

Thanks go for the sharp eyes of my honest friends Dr. Nadine Payn, Dr. Robin Lakoff, Linda Peterson and Marilynn Rowland, for their invaluable comments.

My appreciation to patient friends Janet Falk and Henrietta and Jim Ratcliff, who gave me the space—literally and figuratively—in which to write. And great appreciation to Karen Carlson, Jennifer Navrette and Marsha Sherman—dear friends and walking partners who withstood listening to all my struggles in writing.

To Holly Brady, who made the process of putting this book together in its final form as pain-free and easy as I could have wanted.

My family has as always been there for me, with encouragement and, best of all, with humor.

ABOUT THE AUTHOR

Margret Elson is both a master piano teacher and a psychotherapist.

For over forty years, she has done pioneering work in integrated wellness for performers and artists, presenting her work throughout the United States; in Oslo, Norway; and in London. She has spoken at various conferences, including the Biology of Music-Making (Denver); the First International Conference on Mind, Body and the Performing Arts (New York City); the conference of the Association of Humanistic Psychology (London); and the World Piano Pedagogy Conferences.

Margret's musical background includes ten years as a scholarship student at Juilliard Preparatory Division, where she studied piano with Edgar Roberts, then known as "Mr. Juilliard" for his outstanding teaching. She also studied in the San Francisco Bay Area with Alexander Libermann and Marjorie Petray; and in Paris and New York City. In 1993 she and her piano partner, Elizabeth Swarthout, received a National Endowment of the Arts grant to produce the CD *20th Century American 4-Hand Piano Music* (Laurel Records).

Margret attended Hunter College High School; the University of California, Berkeley, where she received a B.A. and two master's degrees—one in journalism and one in political science; and John F. Kennedy University, where she earned a master's degree in clinical psychology, after which she became a licensed Marriage and Family Therapist.

Combining musical and psychological expertise has led Margret to formulate a unique method for helping musicians and clients integrate technical, physical and emotional ease into their learning processes. Her book *Passionate Practice: The Musician's Guide to Learning, Memorizing and Performing*, which is on the reading list of many conservatory and university music departments, offers musicians a step-by-step process for achieving optimum performance.

Throughout her work, Margret seeks to maintain her sense of humor.

CPSIA information can be obtained
at www.ICGtesting.com
Printed in the USA
FSOW02n1341180917
38599FS

9 780999 117408